WHAT LIFE WAS LIKE

In the Jewel in the Crown

British India
AD 1600 ~ 1905

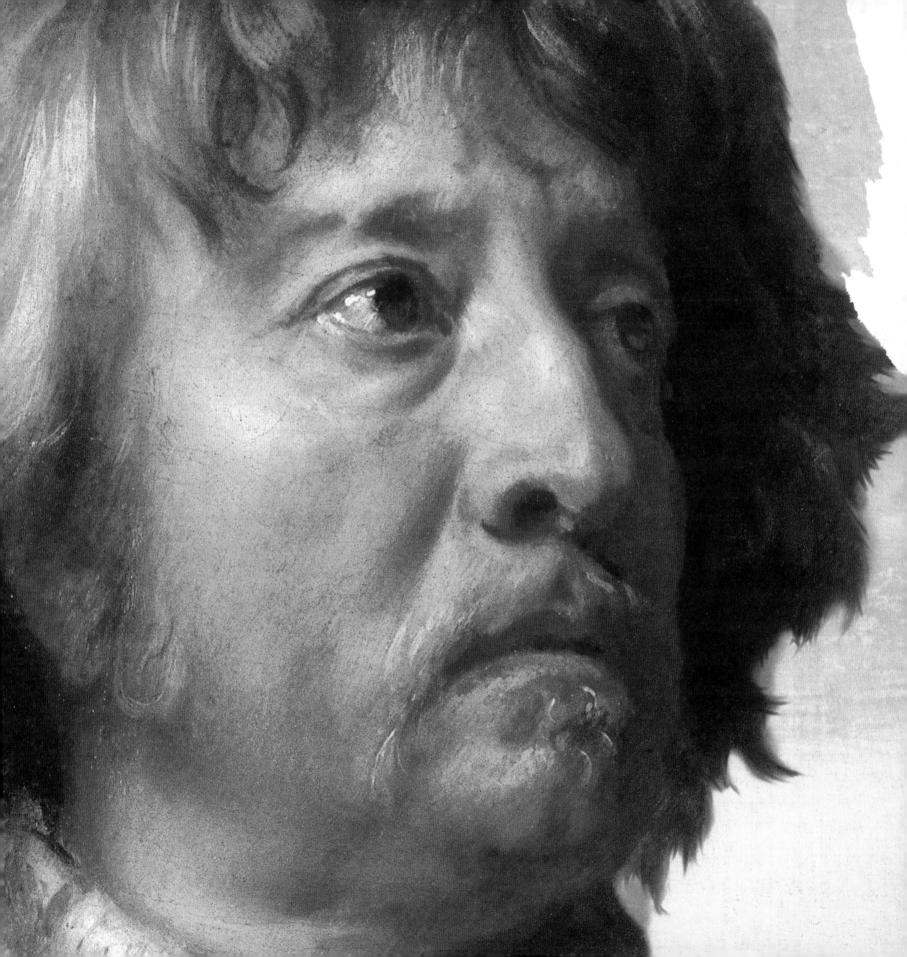

WHAT LIFE WAS LIKE

In the Jewel in the Crown

British India
AD 1600 ~ 1905

by the Editors of Time-Life Books

What Life Was Like
In the Jewel in the Crown

This edition published in 2006
by the Caxton Publishing Group
20 Bloomsbury Street, London WC1B 3JH
Under license from Time-Life Books.

EDITOR: Denise Dersin
DIRECTOR, NEW PRODUCT DEVELOPMENT:
Elizabeth D.Ward
DIRECTOR OF MARKETING:
Pamela R. Farrell

Deputy Editor: Marion Ferguson Briggs
Art Director: Alan Pitts
Text Editor: Jarelle S. Stein
Associate Editor/Research and Writing: Sharon Kurtz Thompson
Senior Copyeditor: Mary Beth Oelkers-Keegan
Technical Art Specialist: John Drummond
Picture Coordinator: David Herod
Editorial Assistant: Christine Higgins

Special Contributors: Anthony Allan, Ronald H. Bailey, Ellen Phillips
(chapter text); Diane Gerard, Christine Hauser, Stacy W. Hoffhaus,
Donna M. Lucey, Marilyn Murphy Terrell, Elizabeth Thompson
(research-writing); Vilasini Balakrishnan, K. Ginger Crockett, Sarah L.
Evans,
Ann-Louise Gates, Beth Levin (research); Janet Cave, Roberta Conlan,
Mimi Harrison (editing); Lina Baber Burton (glossary); Barbara L. Klein
(index and overread).

Correspondents: Christine Hinze (London), Christina Lieberman (New
York), Maria Vincenza Aloisi (Paris). Valuable assistance was also provided by Meenakshi Ganguly (New Delhi).

Director of Finance: Christopher Hearing
Directors of Book Production: Marjann Caldwell, Patricia Pascale
Director of Publishing Technology: Betsi McGrath
Director of Photography and Research: John Conrad Weiser
Director of Editorial Administration: Barbara Levitt
Production Manager: Gertraude Schaefer
Quality Assurance Manager: James King
Chief Librarian: Louise D. Forstall

Title: **What Life Was Like In the Jewel in the Crown**
ISBN: 1 84447 147 0

Consultant:
Rosane Rocher is professor of South Asian Studies and past director
of the National Resource Center for South Asia at the University
of Pennsylvania. Trained as a student of Sanskrit and of classical Indian
culture, she is internationally known as a scholar of the first cultural
and intellectual encounter between India and Europe in the late 18th
and early 19th centuries. Dr. Rocher is the author of several books,
including biographies of two East India Company employees, civil servant Nathaniel B. Halhed and military officer Alexander Hamilton,
whose studies of Indian languages and culture in late-18th-century
Calcutta were seminal for scholarship on India in Britain and continental
Europe.

This volume is one in a series on world history that uses
contemporary art, artifacts, and personal accounts to create
an intimate portrait of daily life in the past.

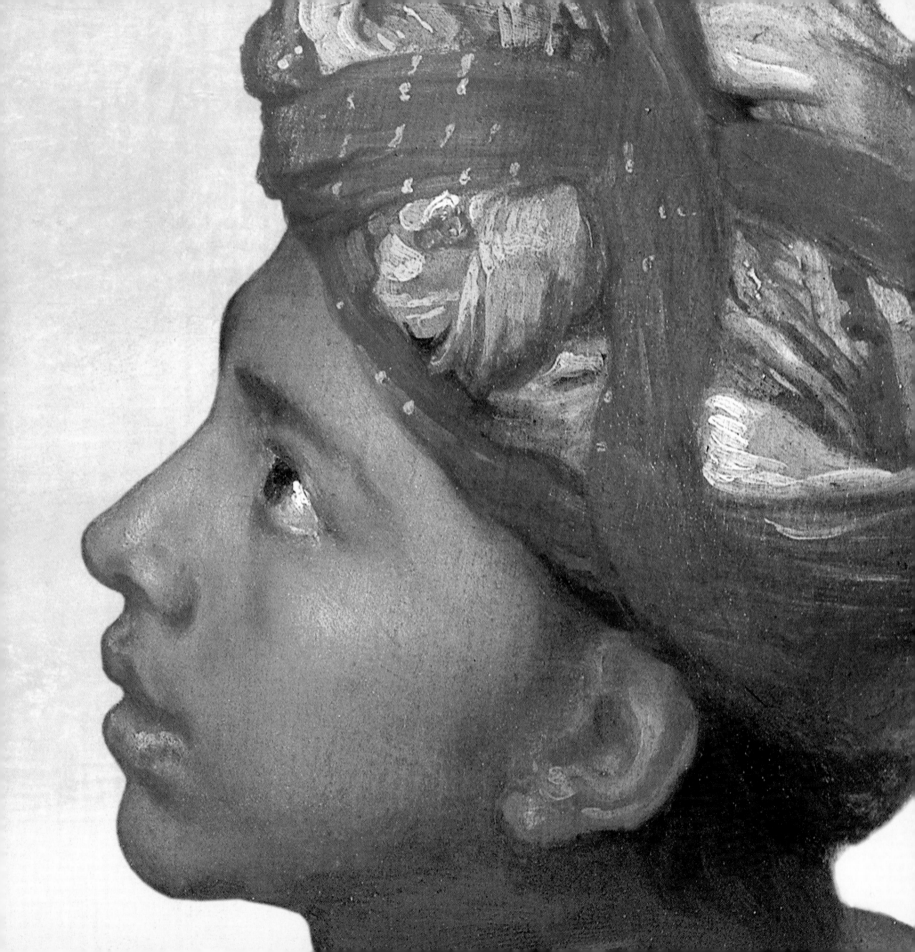

In the Jewel in the Crown

CLAIMING THE BRIGHTEST JEWEL

When traders from England's East India Company arrived on the subcontinent of India in the 17th century, they found a fascinating land of pungent spices and luxurious textiles, magnificent art and architecture, and impressive works of literature and science. By the 19th century, the distant territory shone as the brightest jewel in the British Crown. It remained a prize beyond comparison, valued so highly that, as British viceroy Lord Curzon stated in 1900, "We could lose all our dominions and still survive, but if we lost India, our sun would sink to its setting."

In 1608, when the first East India Company ship weighed anchor off India, the land was dominated in the north by the Moghul empire and ruled in the south by independent Muslim and Hindu kings. With the consent of these rulers, company traders established a handful of small, self-contained posts along the coast and proceeded to vie fiercely with the Portuguese and Dutch for control of the Eastern trading routes.

British-Indian relations often proved contentious as well. In 1686 the East India Company, seeking more control over trade, declared war on Moghul emperor Aurangzeb. The conflict went badly for the Britons, who had to sue for peace in 1690. British relations with the Moghuls were also threatened by European pirates, who trawled the Arabian Sea looking for rich Indian merchant and pilgrim ships. The emperor held the company accountable for all such crimes, thereby forcing its directors to track down and hang buccaneers such as Captain Kidd.

As the 17th century drew to an end, the East

1600
Queen Elizabeth signs charter establishing the East India Company

1608
The first East India Company ship to visit India arrives at Surat

1612
English ships defeat a Portuguese fleet off Surat

1615
Sir Thomas Roe arrives in India as England's ambassador to the Moghul court

1632
Construction begins on the Taj Mahal by order of Moghul emperor Shah Jahan

1640
Fort St. George (Madras) is founded

1661
The Portuguese settlement of Bombay passes into English possession

1686-1690
The East India Company goes to war with Moghul emperor Aurangzeb

1690
Fort William (Calcutta) is founded

1698
Opposition to the East India Company's trade monopoly leads to establishment of the rival New English Company

1708
The rival British companies become the United East India Company

1746
French forces capture Madras and defeat the army of the nawab of the Carnatic

India Company lost its government-granted monopoly on trade in the East, and a rival trading concern was formed. But just 10 years later, the companies joined forces to become the United East India Company. By this time, the hubs of British trade and settlement in India were firmly established—Bombay on the west coast, Madras on the southeast coast, and Calcutta on the Ganges delta in the northeast.

After the death of Emperor Aurangzeb in 1707, the Moghul empire declined. Ensuing conflicts between regional leaders and contenders offered opportunities for Britain and France to seize political and commercial advantage. In 1746 the governor of French Pondicherry on the east coast took Madras and defeated its nawab, supplanting him with a ruler backed by the French. But British forces—with the help of military hero Robert Clive—eventually claimed the throne in 1752 for a British-backed nawab.

British and French ambition worried Siraj-ud-Daula, the nawab of the northeast province of Bengal, who fought back by capturing Fort William at Calcutta in 1756. Clive's troops re-claimed the fortress and defeated Siraj-ud-Daula at the Battle of Plassey. Seven years later, the British defeated Indian forces at the Battle of Buxar and gained the right to collect Bengal's land revenues, making the company the effective ruler of the province.

Clive's actions helped transform the company from a trading concern into a territorial power, collecting land revenue, administering justice, and managing a growing army. But many company officials in Bengal were more interested in getting

1756
Siraj-ud-Daula, nawab of Bengal, seizes Calcutta; British captives are imprisoned overnight in the Black Hole

1757
Robert Clive retakes Calcutta, then defeats Siraj-ud-Daula at Plassey

1764
East India Company troops defeat the nawabs of Bengal and Oudh in the Battle of Buxar

1765
Moghul emperor Shah Alam II turns over to the East India Company the vital function of his *diwan,* or revenue collector, for Bengal, making the British the effective rulers of the province

1767-1769
Haidar Ali, the Muslim ruler of Mysore, and British forces wage the First Anglo-Mysore War

1773
The Regulating Act places the Bombay and Madras presidencies under the authority of the governor of Bengal (henceforth the governor general) and establishes a Supreme Court in Calcutta

1780-1784
Haidar Ali and his son and successor, Tipu Sultan, fight the British in the Second Anglo-Mysore War

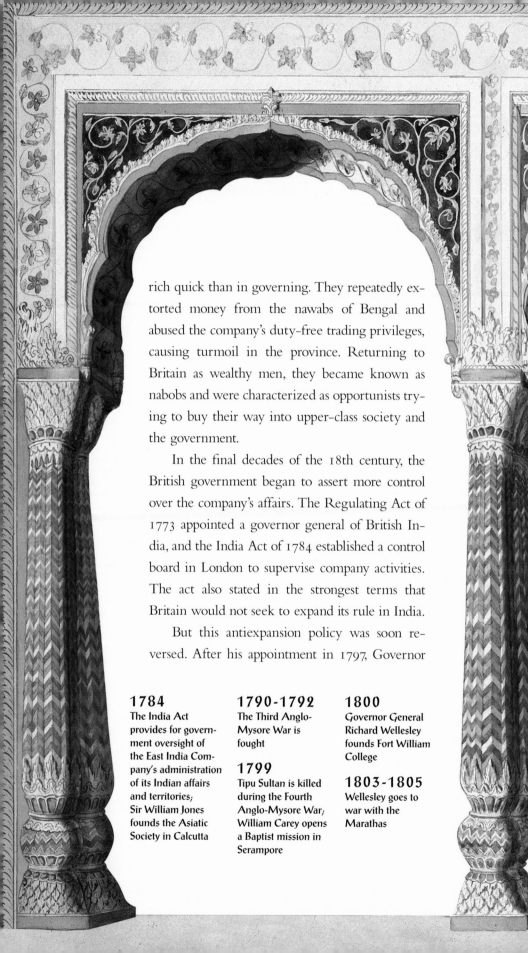

rich quick than in governing. They repeatedly extorted money from the nawabs of Bengal and abused the company's duty-free trading privileges, causing turmoil in the province. Returning to Britain as wealthy men, they became known as nabobs and were characterized as opportunists trying to buy their way into upper-class society and the government.

In the final decades of the 18th century, the British government began to assert more control over the company's affairs. The Regulating Act of 1773 appointed a governor general of British India, and the India Act of 1784 established a control board in London to supervise company activities. The act also stated in the strongest terms that Britain would not seek to expand its rule in India.

But this antiexpansion policy was soon reversed. After his appointment in 1797, Governor

General Richard Wellesley used the instruments of warfare, annexation, and forced alliances to establish British hegemony across most of the subcontinent. Wellesley transformed the company into the paramount power in India, with one of the world's largest standing armies.

At the same time, a British policy of noninterference in Indian religious beliefs and customs gave way to a movement toward Westernization. Beginning with the 1813 charter of the East India Company, the British lifted a ban on missionary activity, promoted Western education and the use of English, and outlawed such religious practices as sati, or widow burning.

The policy of Westernization was introduced during a time of economic turmoil. By the 1820s India's textile industry had been destroyed by imports from British textile mills.

1784
The India Act provides for government oversight of the East India Company's administration of its Indian affairs and territories; Sir William Jones founds the Asiatic Society in Calcutta

1790-1792
The Third Anglo-Mysore War is fought

1799
Tipu Sultan is killed during the Fourth Anglo-Mysore War; William Carey opens a Baptist mission in Serampore

1800
Governor General Richard Wellesley founds Fort William College

1803-1805
Wellesley goes to war with the Marathas

1806
Sepoys at Vellore mutiny; the East India Company opens East India College in England

1809
The East India Company establishes a military college in England

1813
The new East India Company charter permits missionaries to enter India and ends the company's monopoly on Indian trade

1829
Governor General William Bentinck outlaws sati

1835
English replaces Persian as the administrative language; preference established for education in English

1839
Work begins on the Grand Trunk Road from Calcutta to Delhi

Famines, the extension of a rigorous system of tax collection, and displacement of some landowners and peasants by British land reforms added to the distress and discontent.

Westernization continued during the vigorous rule of Lord Dalhousie, governor general from 1848 to 1856. Dalhousie introduced railroads and telegraphs, which would do much to unify India. While Indians appreciated these new technologies, other actions taken by Dalhousie aggravated tensions already mounting between the Indians and Britons. Dalhousie absorbed into the East India Company's domain a number of Indian states, including several where rulers had died without direct heirs.

The growing unrest in India combined with a British disregard for Indian beliefs and customs exploded into the uprising of 1857. Sepoys, disinher-

ited rulers, and other Indians revolted against British rule, and it was not until the following year that the British were able to take back control of all areas. In the aftermath of the uprising, the British Crown assumed governance of India, and in 1877, Queen Victoria was named empress of India.

There were clear signs, however, that India would not stay forever under British rule. Hindus established the Indian National Congress to seek equal rights for Indians in 1885. In 1905 widespread boycotts and protests arose in response to Lord George Curzon's decision to partition Bengal. Three years later, the Muslim League was founded, to make Muslim voices heard, as one member proclaimed, "across the wide seas to England." In the following decades the protests for independence grew until the subcontinent finally brought an end to the British Raj in 1947.

1853
India's first railway line offering passenger service is opened

1856
The British annex the kingdom of Oudh

1857-1858
Indian uprising occurs

1858
The Government of India Act transfers the rule of India from the East India Company to the British Crown

1865
Telegraphic communication between India and Europe begins

1869
The opening of the Suez Canal shortens travel time to India

1877
Queen Victoria's new title, empress of India, is proclaimed at a durbar in Delhi

1885
The Indian National Congress holds its first meeting

1905
Viceroy George Curzon seeks to divide Bengal, causing widespread Indian boycotts and protests

1908
The Muslim League is founded

1947
India is partitioned into India and Pakistan; both gain independence from Britain

Traveling to India from England was a long, tedious, and often dangerous undertaking. Before the 1869 opening of the Suez Canal, most people sailed around Africa's Cape of Good Hope, a voyage of about six months. Ships stopped at islands such as Madeira and St. Helena to take on food and fresh water. Some travelers trekked overland through Vienna to Basra on the Persian Gulf, then boarded a ship for India. Others headed for the Red Sea, either sailing around Spain or journeying overland to Alexandria, Egypt. From Egypt, they crossed the desert by camel to the Red Sea port of Suez, then continued on by ship.

Arriving on the subcontinent *(right)*, Britons found a vast land of more than a million and a half square miles, extending from the Himalayas in the north through the north-central plains to the Deccan plateau in the south. Rivers, including the mighty Ganges, crisscrossed the subcontinent. British trading centers, such as Surat, Bombay, and Madras, proliferated along the west and east coasts. But Calcutta, a beautiful yet tumultuous place that Rudyard Kipling would call "the many-sided, the smoky, the magnificent City of Dreadful Night," became the center of colonial power, the bridgehead of the British in India.

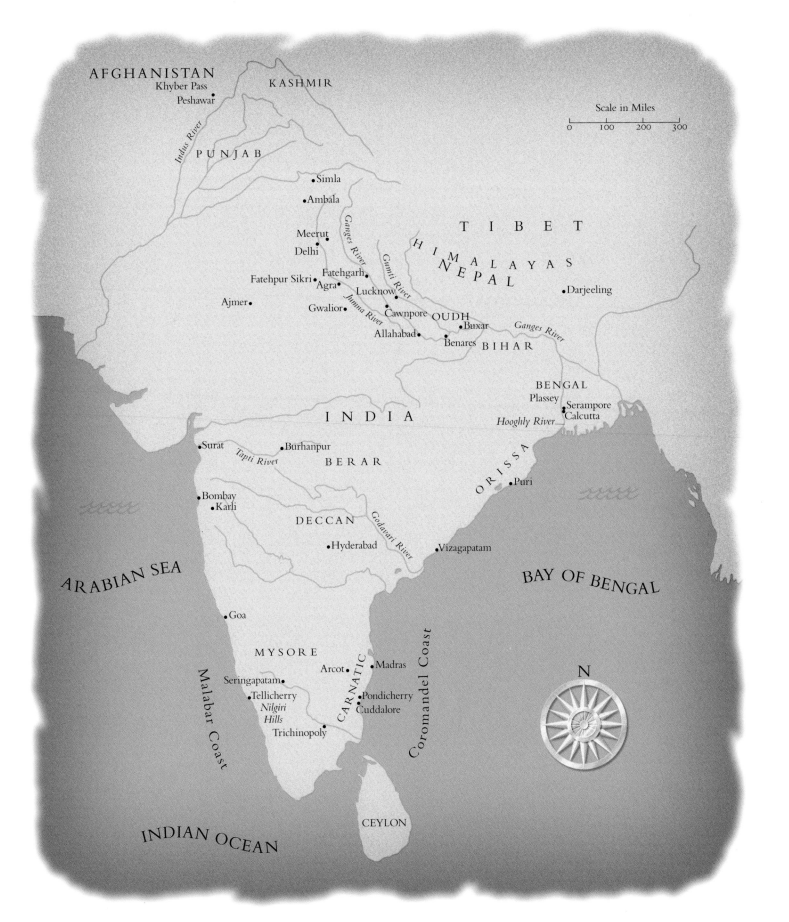

AFGHANISTAN

KASHMIR

Khyber Pass

Peshawar

Indus River

PUNJAB

Simla

Ambala

TIBET

Meerut

Delhi

Ganges River

HIMALAYAS

NEPAL

Fatehpur Sikri

Fatehgarh

Gumti River

Darjeeling

Agra

Lucknow

Ajmer

Gwalior

Jumna River

Cawnpore

OUDH

Allahabad

Buxar

Ganges River

Benares

BIHAR

INDIA

BENGAL

Plassey

Serampore

Calcutta

Hooghly River

Surat

Burhanpur

Tapti River

BERAR

ORISSA

Puri

Bombay

Karli

DECCAN

Godavari River

Hyderabad

Vizagapatam

ARABIAN SEA

BAY OF BENGAL

Goa

MYSORE

CARNATIC

Arcot

Madras

Coromandel Coast

Seringapatam

Tellicherry

Pondicherry

Cuddalore

Nilgiri Hills

Malabar Coast

Trichinopoly

N

CEYLON

INDIAN OCEAN

Scale in Miles

0   100   200   300

The Glory of Moghul India

Centuries before the British ruled India, Muslim armies from central Asia poured through the Khyber Pass and onto the northern plains of the Indian subcontinent. Some of these troops, such as the army of the mighty conqueror Tamerlane, came there to plunder. But in 1526, the army led by Babur, king of Kabul, a descendant of Chinggis Khan and great-grandson of Tamerlane, came there to stay, establishing an empire that would eventually dominate southern Asia. Babur invaded northern India, ransacked Delhi, and set up his capital at Agra, where the seat of the great Moghul empire would remain for much of the two centuries to follow.

Babur's successors expanded and consolidated their hold on India. Akbar, Babur's grand-

son, conquered vast territories and devised a system to oversee his holdings that relied on provincial governors to provide soldiers, keep order, and collect taxes. Akbar, his son Jahangir, and subsequent emperors chose loyal Muslim nobles to serve the empire, but they recruited former Hindu and Muslim adversaries as well.

By the early 1700s the Moghul dynasty ruled more than 100 million people and had become known not only for its military prowess but also for its robust economic policies, elaborate court rituals, and contributions to art and architecture. As with many powerful empires, its authority eventually crumbled. But until the middle of the 18th century, the Moghul empire enjoyed a glorious reign.

Carvings adorn this balcony throne of Akbar's grandson, Emperor Shah Jahan.

Emperor Jahangir welcomes his son, the future emperor Shah Jahan, home from a successful military campaign. Prominent courtiers attend the durbar, or audience, inside the gold railing, while others, including the artist Balchand *(lower left corner)*, who painted this scene in 1635, look on.

In observance of his birthday in 1632, Shah Jahan sits in the pan of a scale to be weighed. His weight in gold and silver was then distributed to the poor.

In a small clearing, Emperor Akbar, on horseback, gores a mother tiger while others attack her cubs in this scene from the *Akbar-nama*, or History of Akbar, written around 1590. Chroniclers kept track of the emperors' successes at the hunt. According to one scribe, Jahangir had killed 86 tigers before he was 50.

Hunters and Warriors

Akbar's youth was spent learning to hunt and fight, skills he used as ruler: His military cunning helped him to expand his empire and his hunting prowess to maintain his hold on the land. Since the emperor's hunting party was composed of a large army and such expeditions doubled as military maneuvers, the sight of Akbar and his troops on the hunt for elephant, tiger, and other game had the effect of quelling rebellion in his territories.

Hunts typically lasted for about a week—although Akbar's son Jahangir once spent more than three months on the hunt. Military campaigns, by contrast, were long and bloody and could take years to complete. While Akbar led his army in person, later emperors often sent their soldiers out under the command of their sons. The princes gained experience they could later put to good use: Moghul emperors, following Islamic practice, did not name a successor, which often led to battles between brothers.

This shield, decorated with the signs of the zodiac, and punch dagger, its blade inlaid with black lacquer and its hilt with gold, are ornate versions of the traditional weapons carried by Moghul soldiers.

Under cannon fire from men loyal to a renegade Moghul official, Emperor Shah Jahan's soldiers scale the walls of Fort Dharur in 1631, during his campaign in the Deccan, the central plateau of southern India.

17

Religious Discord

When Akbar became emperor, Muslim law ruled the land. Non-Muslims were taxed, and fees were levied on pilgrims traveling to Hindu shrines and festivals. But the emperor needed the support of the powerful Hindu nobles to control his largely non-Muslim empire, and despite opposition from orthodox Muslim leaders, Akbar liberalized laws and repealed the taxes that had penalized Hindus. These moves earned the emperor popular support, and after Akbar's death, his son Jahangir continued his father's policies.

Subsequent emperors were not as liberal, however, and began a return to strict Islamic rule. Jahangir's son Shah Jahan prohibited repair or new construction of Hindu temples and destroyed those temples not yet completed. His son, Aurangzeb, who became emperor after executing his eldest brother (who had sought to fuse Islam and Hinduism), married only Muslims and reinstated taxes on Hindus. Court musicians and artists were dismissed, and non-Islamic ceremonies and celebrations were banned.

The Pearl Mosque *(below),* built by Emperor Aurangzeb in 1659 inside the fort at Delhi, was used for private worship. Black marble inlay divides the floor into individual areas of prayer around the *minbar,* or pulpit (partially hidden by arch), from which sermons would be delivered.

Shah Jahan honors Muslim religious leaders at a candlelight feast in these painted panels dating from 1635. Although the emperor initiated a return to Muslim law, he continued to patronize Hindu musicians and artists.

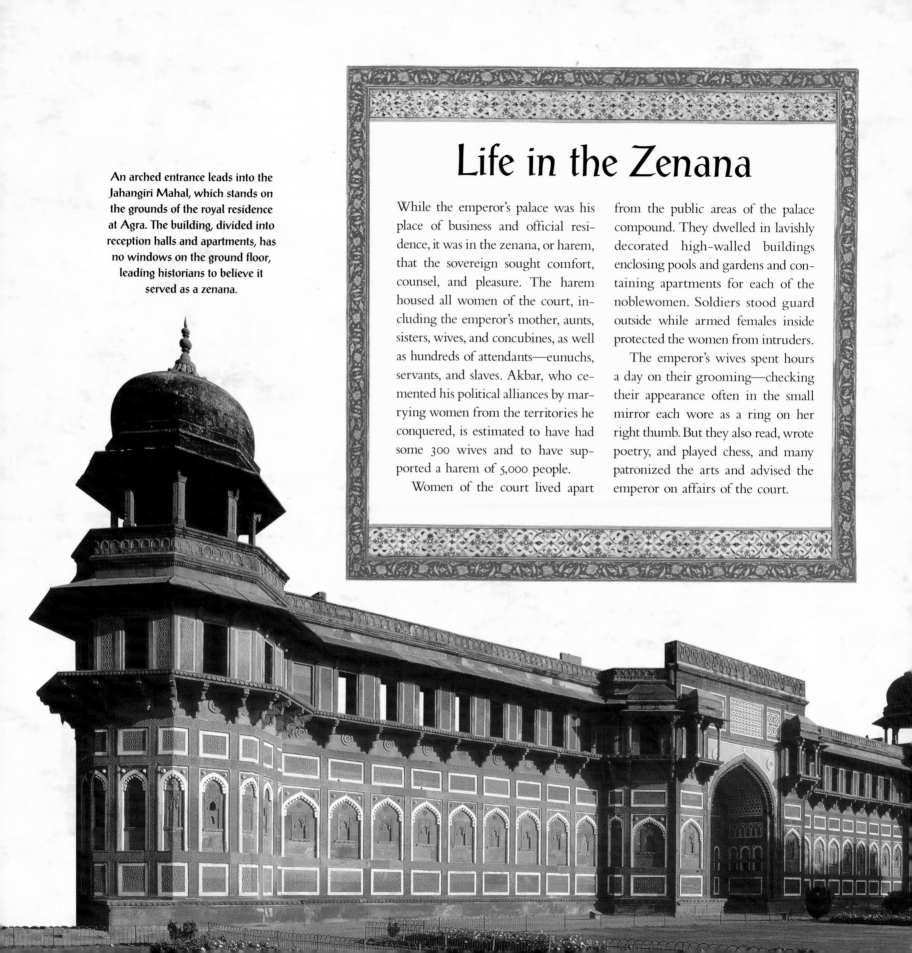

An arched entrance leads into the Jahangiri Mahal, which stands on the grounds of the royal residence at Agra. The building, divided into reception halls and apartments, has no windows on the ground floor, leading historians to believe it served as a zenana.

Life in the Zenana

While the emperor's palace was his place of business and official residence, it was in the zenana, or harem, that the sovereign sought comfort, counsel, and pleasure. The harem housed all women of the court, including the emperor's mother, aunts, sisters, wives, and concubines, as well as hundreds of attendants—eunuchs, servants, and slaves. Akbar, who cemented his political alliances by marrying women from the territories he conquered, is estimated to have had some 300 wives and to have supported a harem of 5,000 people.

Women of the court lived apart from the public areas of the palace compound. They dwelled in lavishly decorated high-walled buildings enclosing pools and gardens and containing apartments for each of the noblewomen. Soldiers stood guard outside while armed females inside protected the women from intruders.

The emperor's wives spent hours a day on their grooming—checking their appearance often in the small mirror each wore as a ring on her right thumb. But they also read, wrote poetry, and played chess, and many patronized the arts and advised the emperor on affairs of the court.

Attended by servants bearing trays of sweets and drinks, Queen Nur Jahan entertains her husband, Emperor Jahangir, and his son Khurram, the future Shah Jahan, on a garden terrace in the zenana in this miniature from around 1800.

Accompanied by veiled attendants, a lady of the court travels in a closed palanquin in this late-16th-century painting. Select members of the harem accompanied the emperor on his travels, camping in their own elaborate tent compound.

Emperor Akbar *(top, in white)* inspects the building of his red sandstone palace city, Fatehpur Sikri. Begun in 1571, the city's buildings—including the royal residence, harem, and mosque—combined elements of Indian and Persian architecture.

In a garden at dusk with guests and servants, a Moghul prince enjoys a poetry reading, accompanied by music and refreshments. The Moghul court supported poets, historians, philosophers, and theologians, who wrote and translated a wide range of books into Persian, the official court language.

A Legacy in Art and Architecture

"There are many that hate painting," Emperor Akbar once commented, "but such men I dislike." The wealth and resources of the Moghul emperors, and their genuine interest in the arts and architecture, initiated a fertile period of scholarly and artistic development. Scholars, painters, poets, and artisans from all over India and Persia were welcomed at court.

The early Moghul rulers also initiated a distinct style of architecture, often incorporating a garden in the plan for a building. Gardens typically were symmetrical in layout and included fountains or flowing water. Later emperors combined Persian architectural elements such as domes, vaults, and arches with Indian rooftop pavilions and covered balconies.

Inside, the walls of the emperors' palaces were carved and set with inlays of lapis lazuli, jade, carnelian, and other semiprecious stones to create intricate flower motifs. In Islamic cultures, flowers symbolize the divine realm.

Inlaid stones in floral and geometric patterns, relief carvings, and calligraphic panels embellish the white marble of the Taj Mahal. Begun by Shah Jahan in 1632 and taking nearly two decades to complete, it served as a tomb for his beloved wife Mumtaz Mahal.

CHAPTER ONE

Drawn to India's Shores

English merchant ships anchor at the East India Company factory in the southwest Indian port of Tellicherry, famed as a trading center for pepper and cardamom. The British first sailed to India as company traders in the early 17th century, opening the way for thousands of their compatriots, who would change as well as be changed by life on the subcontinent.

 ith cannon booming and red, white, and blue flags and pennants flying, the four British ships anchored off India's northwest coast on September 26, 1615, heralded the arrival of a royal ambassador to the Moghul empire. A fanfare of trumpets rang out in counterpoint from one of two boats heading toward shore. In the other craft rode the ambassador, Sir Thomas Roe, accompanied by several naval officers and merchants. A tall man of 35 with an impressive mustache and goatee, Roe contemplated the approaching beach and his reasons for braving a six-month voyage to reach it.

Roe's mission, as noted in the letter he carried from King James, was to petition the Moghul emperor for a treaty granting "quiet Trade and Commerce without any kind of hindrance or molestation." India, with its rich and varied textiles, spices, indigo, sugar, and saltpeter, promised unparalleled trading opportunities for Roe's employer, the English East India Company. At present, the company had a few trading stations, or factories, on the subcontinent but no formal agreement granting British rights to trade there. The company directors had sent other men to petition the emperor for such an agreement; they had all failed.

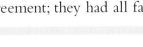

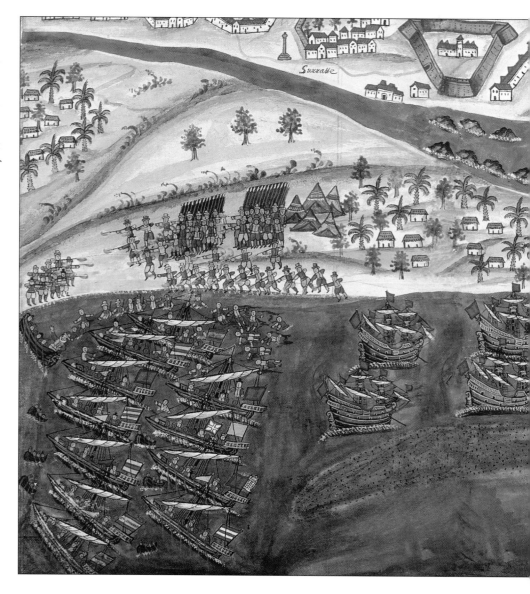

Reaching shore, the new ambassador stepped smartly onto Indian soil and through the ranks of an honor guard of 80 British seamen armed with pikes and muskets—then drew up short. He could see the city officials from nearby Surat awaiting him beneath a large tent. But instead of standing in his honor, they remained seated on their carpets. Roe spoke to one of his men, who hastened ahead to inform the officials that they must rise for King James's representative. They complied, and Roe entered the tent.

Another problem soon emerged. The officials informed Roe that he and his entourage would have to submit their belongings and their persons to the usual customs search. Offended, Sir Thomas exclaimed that he "would never dishonour my master" by submitting to such an indignity. When his hosts insisted, Roe turned on his heel and returned to his ship. A compromise finally exempted Roe and five of his men from the search. The rest of his company would merely be embraced, an act that could be interpreted as either a gesture of courtesy or a search.

The pomp of Roe's introduction and his demand for deference were carefully calculated. In his opinion, his predecessors had allowed themselves to be humiliated, one representative letting his group be "very familiarly searched all of us to the bottom of our pockets." These earlier petitioners from the company had not been accredited by the king and were scorned by the Moghul court as mere merchants. Since those men had claimed ambassador status, the Moghuls had formed a poor opinion of England and its ruler. "The king's honour was engaged more deeply than I did expect," Roe wrote. Success in his mission, the royal ambassador believed, hinged upon his ability to engender respect for himself and his kingdom, and he "was resolved either to rectify all or lay my life and fortune both on the ground."

In an early-17th-century battle for control of trade near Surat, India, Dutch crews from five warships fire on Portuguese galleons *(above).* Europeans vied fiercely for the East Indies' spice routes in a competition that was often cruel as well as violent, as portrayed at right in an illustration of a British merchant's torture by the Dutch in Indonesia.

Thomas Roe, observed an East India Company official, was a gentleman "of a pregnant understanding, well spoken, learned, industrious and of a comely personage." Born into a prominent merchant family that produced three lord mayors of London, Roe had studied at Oxford's Magdalen College, served as a courtier to Queen Elizabeth and King James, who had knighted him, and held a seat in Parliament. He had even commanded an expedition up South America's Amazon River. Married since then, he needed money and was delighted to accept the ambassador's post and the salary that went with it.

Mounting horses provided by the local officials, Roe and some of his men rode ahead to the bustling mercantile city of Surat, site of the company's most important factory. The city, they discovered, was protected on the southwest by a stone-and-burnt-brick fort and the winding Tapti River and on its other sides by earthen walls. Just beyond the fort, haggling over goods in the open-air bazaar, were buyers and sellers from not only India and England, but Turkey, Persia, and Armenia, as well as Portugal and the Netherlands. In their European clothing, the new arrivals stood out in the sea of loose white cotton garments worn by most of those present, sensible dress in Surat's tropical climate.

Roe had arrived just as the wet, or monsoon, season had given way to the cool season. With the better weather came ships in greater numbers, stopping in Surat before sailing on to other Indian and foreign ports. At the same time, large caravans of oxcarts and camels loaded with goods set out for the country's interior. Such trade had brought prosperity to some of Surat's residents, whose brick-and-lime houses, graced by bamboo curtains and even a few glass windows, presented a sharp contrast to the reed houses of the poorer citizens.

Surat's affluence was of recent origin. Though Asian ships had frequented the port before the appearance of the Portuguese and Dutch, it was the Europeans' arrival in the early 16th century that caused trade there to explode. Spices and other goods from the East Indies (an area extending from India to modern-day Indonesia) were highly profitable for Europeans, who struggled fiercely for control of the trade. Portugal's hold was strongest in India, while the Dutch dominated in Indonesia. Around 1600, the British entered the fray, vying in both arenas.

Roe would call Surat "the fountain and life of all the East India trade." But right now, he wanted nothing more than to leave it behind and press on to Ajmer, to make his case with the Moghul

As ambassador to the Moghul court, Sir Thomas Roe always dressed in English style and required his staff to wear red taffeta cloaks in public, even in hot weather.

emperor. The Portuguese wanted to undermine the British, who threatened their decades-long dominance of Arabian Sea trade routes. The East India Company had managed to gain a foothold in the Moghul empire in 1612 when their small, swift, and heavily gunned ships repulsed a larger Portuguese fleet just off Surat. The demonstration of sea power had impressed the Moghul rulers, who wanted to protect the ships full of pilgrims crossing the Arabian Sea to Mecca from European pirates. The Portuguese had provided such defense, but the Moghuls did not always get along with them. Lately, however, relations had been improving. A Portuguese representative at the imperial court, backed by powerful Moghul bureaucrats, had drafted an agreement that would ban British trade altogether. The emperor had not signed it yet; Roe wanted to make sure he never did.

Hostile relations with officials in Surat delayed the ambassador for five weeks. First there were hassles over customs inspections and the landing and confiscation of English goods, then an argument with the governor over which of them would pay the first courtesy visit. Roe protested every challenge, finally sending a letter to a company representative at the Moghul court, asking him to apprise Emperor Jahangir of the situation. The emperor sent an order forbidding Indian governors to interfere with the English-

man. Triumphant, Roe packed his carts, hired guards to protect his train from bandits, and set out.

The arduous 600-mile journey to the court at Ajmer took nearly two months. Roe and his party traveled due east to the city of Burhanpur before turning north toward Ajmer. It was longer, but safer, than a direct route, and in Burhanpur, the British could pay their respects to the emperor's second son, Parwiz. Roe plied the prince with gifts and came away with a firman, or edict, allowing the company to set up a factory in the city, which was linked to Surat by the Tapti River. The Englishman also came away with a raging fever. "I am here visited by God's hand with a terrible fever," he wrote, "not able to walk two turns in my tent." Roe had to be carried in a palanquin, or covered litter, for the journey's final leg. Reaching Ajmer at last, he spent nearly three weeks recuperating.

At 4 p.m. on January 10, 1616, Roe finally presented himself at court in the yellow stone fort that served as the imperial residence. It was the beginning of the durbar, a daily two-hour period during which the emperor made an appearance, the Englishman noted, "to entertain strangers, to receive petitions and presents, to give commands, to see, and to be seen." People stood on three levels, separated by railings: the ordinary folks on the ground, those of higher rank on a slightly raised platform, and the top nobles and visitors on a richly carpeted higher platform under canopies of velvet and silk. Overhead, on a little balcony attended by two eunuchs with fans, sat Emperor Jahangir, whose

The haloed Emperor Jahangir, often called Light of Religion, gives his attention to a cleric while ignoring both a Turkish sultan and James I *(bottom left)*. James's image was copied from a portrait thought to be a gift from Sir Thomas Roe.

name meant Conqueror of the World. Jahangir presided over some 100 million subjects in an empire that embraced modern-day Afghanistan, Pakistan, and all of northern and central India.

Flanked by two slaves, Roe began his walk toward the emperor. Concerned, perhaps, that he might be expected to prostrate himself before the monarch, Roe had gained permission beforehand to make a suitable "reverence" according to English, not Moghul, customs. At each railing, he stopped and bowed low. At the innermost railing, Roe looked up and offered his royal credentials. Through an interpreter who translated the court language of Persian, Jahangir welcomed his visitor and reassured him that the Moghul emperor and the English king "were brothers." Roe then presented the gifts he had brought, including a handsome closed carriage complete with English coachman. The emperor was "so fond of the coach," Roe observed, "that at night in his court he got into it, and made two or three of my men draw him a little in it." Jahangir was also taken with a gift sword, which he tied on his waist with a scarf and "marched up and down, drawing it and flourishing."

Roe's first, favorable impressions of the Moghul ruler never changed. "Very affable, and of a cheerful countenance, without pride," the ambassador noted, and "full of gentle conversation." Jahangir, who was in his late forties, had succeeded his father, the great Akbar, a decade previously. He was excessively fond of drink and of his many wives and concubines, sometimes lax in duties of state, and occasionally given to outbursts of cruelty. After his eldest son attempted a coup, Jahangir had more than 300 of the prince's followers massacred and the prince partially blinded and imprisoned. At the same time, the emperor possessed a powerful curiosity about science and nature, recording his perceptions in a daily journal. Court painters blossomed under Jahangir's patronage, producing exquisite portraiture. The emperor's desire for a visual record of plant and animal life also fostered an inventive new realism among the painters.

Jahangir, for his part, admired the English ambassador's sober demeanor and high principles. Yet he proved utterly indifferent to Roe's mission. Though the emperor quashed the idea of expelling the British factors, as the company agents were known, trade with England did not interest him greatly. The island kingdom did not produce anything his people wanted, other than silver. A formal treaty, as opposed to the less binding imperial edict, seemed contrary to the dignity and grandeur of the imperial court.

Roe, in his quest for a binding trade agreement, soon discovered that the emperor was surrounded by a powerful clique opposed to extending British trading privileges. At the center was Jahangir's favorite wife, Nur Jahan. Since by custom women of rank did not appear in public, Roe never saw her. But she was reputed to be beautiful as well as intelligent, an accomplished poet, a keen hunter of tigers, and the power behind the throne. Her formidable influence was reinforced by her father, the emperor's chief minister; her brother, a key minister; his daughter, wife of the emperor's favorite son, Khurram; and the prince himself, viceroy of the province that included Surat. This quintet was devoted to advancing the prince's claim to succeed his father and feared that friendly relations with England would alienate the powerful Portuguese.

Life in the East India Company

On a blustery day in February 1601, four trading ships set sail from England, bound for the East Indies. The venture's sponsors were unaware that this, the East India Company's maiden voyage, would lead to the formation of a great trading network centered on the subcontinent of India.

As the company discovered over the years, operating so far from home required the establishment of factories, or trading stations, in the larger ports of call. In India, factories attracted local brokers and overland and maritime traders, including textile merchants from the interior and coffee traders from the Persian Gulf. Company agents, known as factors, also contracted for the regular delivery of goods from outlying areas to ensure that a ready supply of merchandise was available whenever company ships arrived in port. Contracting also avoided last-minute haggling with brokers about price.

England's first Indian factory was at Surat, on the northwest coast. Bombay, to the south, eventually replaced Surat as the main trading center on the west coast. On the east coast, the fortified factories at Madras and Calcutta emerged as the preeminent centers of trade. Initially, Bombay, Madras, and Calcutta operated independently of each other, under the direction of a local president and a council of senior merchants. The

Indian merchants gather outside the East India Company factory in the Indian town of Surat *(above)*, called "the storehouse of all India." Later factories were forts, near which Indians built towns.

In a highly stylized vignette from fabric painted by an Indian artist, European merchants chat in the garden of an ornate factory *(left)* while Indian brokers wait outside beneath a flag *(far left)*. In Bombay, merchants traded with Bombay rupees such as those shown at right, minted by the East India Company beginning in 1678, under the authority of King Charles II.

At the docks in London, barrels, boxes, and bundles of goods unloaded from East India Company ships wait to be carted to warehouses located in the gardens behind the nearby headquarters of the East India Company.

In the salesroom inside company headquarters in London, prospective buyers bid on goods during a 19th-century auction. One observer called the "howling and yelling" of the buyers and sellers "quite frightful."

three presidents, who also presided over smaller factories in the surrounding areas, reported directly to London.

By 1710 the company was dispatching 10 to 15 ships east each year, some traveling as far as China to acquire tea, one of the company's most profitable imports. A round-trip voyage to India typically took a year and a half, including time spent unloading and loading goods and waiting for favorable winds. Ships usually left England in fall or winter and arrived in India—if all went well—about six months later, ahead of the monsoons that usually began in June. The ships then left India early in the new year to catch the trade winds around the Cape of Good Hope and avoid arriving in England in winter.

In England, ships docked at the East India Company wharves in London, where the cargoes of imported goods were unloaded and readied for sale. Company officials held regularly scheduled auctions for wholesalers, who came from all over England and Europe. Separate auctions were held for each commodity; auctions could run for as long as a week. The goods were then moved out of the company warehouses and sold throughout the country to individual buyers, greatly changing what the British ate and the way they dressed.

Roe found that the surest way to get the emperor's attention was with gifts that arrived with the company's fleet. Jahangir, though rich beyond measure, was so eager to get his hands on the presents that one year he confiscated the cases. To Roe's fury, he appropriated everything for himself, even gifts planned for others at court and a hat intended for the ambassador's own head. Most of all, Jahangir wanted a huge English horse. He suggested to Roe that if six horses were shipped, one might survive the journey. Two English mastiffs did survive the trip, and the emperor assigned four attendants to each dog—two to carry the animal on a palanquin, and two to fan it.

Jahangir liked paintings best of all. Discovering the Englishman had a handsome miniature of his wife, Jahangir had five copies made by court painters, so his principal wives would each wear one. Roe presented the emperor with another miniature, boasting that only a European could have painted such a masterpiece. Jahangir had his own painters make duplicates of it and then challenged Roe to pick the original from among them. The Englishman had a difficult time of it. "You see," said Jahangir, "we are not so unskillful as you esteem us."

Roe and the company were disappointed that Jahangir did not adopt the customary European practice of paying the visiting ambassador's household expenses. From time to time, the emperor did send to Roe's residence a wild pig and other large game he had killed while hunting. He also presented the ambassador with a suspected felon to serve as his male slave and with a female slave. Roe accepted the man as a servant, but returned the woman. Royal generosity, Roe grumbled, thus far had consisted of "hog's flesh, deer, a thief and a whore." Despite Roe's complaints, Jahangir undoubtedly had offered the ambassador presents he considered suitable to the Englishman's rank.

Still, in pursuit of his treaty, Roe would suffer any number of slights and hardships. He followed Jahangir as the emperor traveled throughout the empire, living in thatched huts with mud walls that threatened to wash away in the monsoon rains. He contended with dysentery and suffered exposure to the plague that claimed seven men in his party. And a lion ate his pet dog. But despite more than three years of resolute effort, Roe did not get the coveted formal treaty.

Yet the ambassador accomplished much. He helped open up profitable company commerce with Persia, as well as with Mocha and other Red Sea ports. He also provided a good deal of sound advice to the East India Company. Avoid building land-based military garrisons like those of the Portuguese, he counseled, because the costs "will eat the Profit." Instead, he said, "Let this be received as a rule that if you will profit seek it at sea and in quiet trade"— engage in peaceful commerce backed by English naval power.

As Roe waited in Surat early in 1619 for his homeward-bound ship, he was treated with a respect and courtesy that contrasted sharply with his chilly welcome years before. He had in his pocket a special firman from his former antagonist Prince Khurram. This edict strengthened the position of the company factors in Surat, who could now trade, bear arms, and govern their lives without interference. He also carried a cordial letter from Emperor Jahangir to King James. The Moghul ruler promised fair treatment for British merchants and freedom of movement for their ships. For England's king himself, Jahangir sent two antelopes, a tent, and several beautiful carpets.

Sir Thomas Roe sailed home with the letter and gifts and went on to a successful diplomatic career that carried him throughout Europe. But his greatest achievement remained what he had accomplished in faraway India. Thousands of British men and women would follow him there in the coming decades. Some would journey to the subcontinent to marvel at the wonders of a foreign land. Many would go hoping to get rich—from trade or plunder. Others would find themselves there with muskets on their shoulders as Europe's wars spilled into India. And ne'er-do-well sons, as well as daughters and nieces with poor marriage prospects in England, would be shipped off with their parents' hopes that they would succeed abroad as they never had at home. For all of them, Sir Thomas Roe had set the stage, fostering the conditions under which British influence could eventually take hold and prevail on Indian soil.

In the decades between Roe's mission and the century's end, succeeding Moghul emperors and other local rulers allowed the East India Company to establish more factories along the subcontinent's coasts. Rivalry with the Portuguese declined, but fierce competition raged on with the Dutch and then the French. To disrupt the trade of their rivals, European governments authorized privateers to prey on each other's ships for profit, but many treasure hunters scorned even that veneer of legitimacy. All manner of European pirates descended on the Arabian Sea to plunder merchant ships and the fleets of rich pilgrims bound to and from Mecca. The East India Company soon discovered that piracy threatened the company's very future on the subcontinent.

In September 1695 pirate ships under notorious English buccaneer Henry Avery attacked the pilgrim fleet off India's west coast. The pirates boarded the *Ganj-i-Sawai,* an enormous ship belonging to Moghul emperor Aurangzeb himself that carried both pilgrims and treasure. The buccaneers plundered the gold and silver and tortured and raped pilgrims—among them, by one account, the emperor's daughter. Learning the pirates' nationality, Aurangzeb imprisoned every Englishman in Surat. Only after the company agreed to provide safe escort for the pilgrim fleet—and paid ransom—were the prisoners released. It was clear to every British mariner and factor that if another such incident should occur, Aurangzeb would probably banish the company from his empire.

On June 14, 1697, English mariner Edward Barlow felt the heavy weight of preventing that possibility drop onto his shoulders. Standing on the *Sceptre*, he watched the lead-weighted coffin bearing his captain's body sink beneath the waves of the Arabian Sea. The captain had taken ill and died the night before, and as chief mate, Barlow was next in line to take over the ship's command and mission. The East India Company vessel, along with two Dutch ships, had been dispatched to the Red Sea port of Mocha to rendezvous with a fleet of pilgrims—and the Indian merchants who traveled with them to trade cotton textiles and spices for coffee and gold. The convoy's assignment was simple: Protect the fleet on the 2,000-mile return voyage to Surat at all costs.

A yearning to see "strange things in other countries" had first drawn the now 55-year-old Barlow to the sea. Son of a debt-ridden farmer near Manchester, he had been so poor as a child that he had no "clothes fitting to go to church in." At age 15, reacting against the provincialism of neighbors who "would not venture a day's journey from out of the smoke of their chimneys," he ran away to London. There he saw his first ships and, not long after, apprenticed himself to the chief mate of a Royal Navy man-of-war. In 1669 he joined the East India Company's merchant fleet, working his way up the ranks. But he despaired of ever reaching the top. He was too poor— captains typically had to purchase the position from shipowners—and too plain spoken: Twice he had been thrown off ships for quarreling with the

Sails billowing, flags flying, and cannon at the ready, the Indiaman *Sceptre* travels the seas in this illustration from Edward Barlow's journal. Barlow, who captained the *Sceptre*, began keeping a journal, complete with drawings, while a Dutch prisoner in Indonesia during the 1670s.

commander. Now fortune had intervened, and Barlow had his command. Whether the company let him keep it remained to be seen.

Four days after the burial at sea, the *Sceptre* reached the port of Mocha. The voyage had been grueling and perilous, the ship constantly tossed by rough waters and gales and buffeted by counter winds. Reaching Mocha intact had been a true feat, one appreciated by local residents. When Barlow and the ship's purser went ashore to begin trade negotiations, a group of boys serenaded them. As the new captain noted in his journal, "The tune was only our welcome for our safe arrival there at such a season, as none had done the like before."

Though the *Sceptre* had been sent to escort pilgrims, trade could not be neglected. The financial survival of an Indiaman (as ships working for the company were known) depended on trade. Barlow discharged the *Sceptre's* cargo of sugar, pepper, rice, knives, scissors, lead, and iron. He took on some spices, dyes, and ivory but mainly he loaded on board the commodity for which Mocha was becoming world-renowned—coffee.

As he waited for the pilgrim fleet to arrive from Mecca, farther north, Barlow spent time in Mocha, with its whitewashed sea front and imposing mosque minarets and cosmopolitan population that included Syrian, Armenian, Jewish, and Indian traders. A wealthy Indian Muslim merchant invited Barlow and the Dutch commanders to dinner. "He provided a great deal of good victuals," the English captain wrote, "but they used no tables but spread a carpet and sat all round on their heels, which we could not very well do, being not used to such fashions."

By the time the *Sceptre,* the two Dutch vessels, and the 17 pilgrim ships sailed on August 11, 1697, rumors of a pirate ship marauding nearby had reached Barlow. The pirates reportedly had gone ashore at an island to the southwest of Mocha, made off with cattle, and killed some inhabitants. They were said to be lurking there among the islands near the mouth of the Red Sea, where the convoy would have to pass southward through the narrow strait of Bab al-mandab. The two Dutch ships together mounted 60 guns, but Barlow distrusted these temporary allies. Many Indians believed all pirates were British, and Barlow was aware that the Dutch might easily use another attack to discredit their rivals. So he counted on his ship alone, a strongly constructed Indiaman with two decks and 36 cannon.

On August 14 Barlow and his convoy slipped quietly through the strait in the dead of night. His crew, tense and alert, scanned the water, ready to give cry at the first sign of an unknown ship. But their passage remained clear, and with a sigh of relief, they sailed

In another Barlow sketch, a rhinoceros stands near the town of Hooghly and the Hooghly River, location of several European factories. In 1683 Edward Barlow made his way to Bengal, in northeast India, after being dismissed from a ship at Sumatra. While awaiting passage home, the ever-curious Barlow gathered information on Bengal's customs, trade, and animals.

out of the strait unscathed. Relief proved premature. Standing on deck the next morning, eyes sweeping the Muslim fleet, Barlow realized something was wrong: He counted 18, not 17, ships. And on the masthead of the 18th vessel flew the blood-red banner of a pirate ship.

Despite the light wind, the intruder was swiftly bearing down on its prey under its two topsails. Worse still, the pirate vessel, unlike Barlow's, contained a row of openings on its lower gun deck for oars, which could be used to propel the vessel during calm weather. The English ship, sporting sails alone, had no such maneuverability. Yet Barlow held one advantage: surprise. The *Sceptre* flags had not been hoisted, and nothing identified her from afar as a British Indiaman—a more formidable foe than the pilgrims. Hoping the pirates might mistake the *Sceptre* for a Muslim vessel, the captain held his fire and waited. When the enemy ship came almost abreast, Barlow "let fly two or three guns at him." The battle for the fleet was on.

The British shots missed; the pirate ship was still out of range. His sails useless, Barlow yelled for men to launch the boats. With towlines attached, the boat crews strained to pull the Indiaman along behind them and close the distance. Meanwhile, the buccaneers turned their guns on a Muslim vessel, putting shots through hull and sails. Barlow, colors now flying, fired again and ordered all available crewmen aloft into the rigging to shout threats and curses at the enemy—an old pirate trick aimed at cowing the target into submission. The strategy paid off. Breaking out their oars, the pirates veered away.

As the day progressed, the buccaneer ship lurked in the vicinity, clearly hoping to catch a straggler. A determined Barlow continued to challenge it. Finally conceding defeat, the intruder made sail and disappeared. It was, the English captain concluded, "a good piece of service done for the company's interest."

Barlow would not learn until later that his adversary had been William Kidd. Born in Scotland the son of a rigid Calvinist minister, the violent-tempered Kidd originally had pursued a career as commander of privateers. In 1691 he married a wealthy widow in New York and settled down for a time. Eventually restless again for action, he obtained the backing of powerful politicians in England—and the formal approval of King William III—for a privateering voyage against pirates and French shipping in the East. He sailed his newly launched privateer back to New York, then a notorious haven for pirates, where he filled out his crew with what New York's governor described as "men of desperate fortunes and necessitous of getting vast treasure." En route to catch buccaneers, Kidd turned pirate himself and headed for the Red Sea and the pilgrim fleet. "Come boys," he told his eager crew, "I will make money enough out of that fleet!"

Edward Barlow thwarted those plans and, 26 days later, led his convoy safely to Surat. The company factors there had been fearfully awaiting the pilgrim fleet's arrival, expecting to be thrown into prison again "if any of the [Muslims] had come short home." Vastly relieved, they invited Barlow for a festive evening ashore. The commanders of two other Indiamen joined in. "We were very merry with our countrymen and women, which were seven in all, dancing and making great mirth in an evening."

Pirate raids and escort duty behind them, the *Sceptre* resumed hauling cargo. The ship sailed down the coast to Bombay, the island that in 1661 had been given to English king Charles II, who had turned it over to the company. Here Barlow's promotion to captain was officially confirmed. "It pleased the [governor of Bombay] to declare me amongst our ship's company commander of the ship *Sceptre*," wrote Barlow, who certainly was pleased himself.

The ship continued on to the southwest part of the subcontinent, the Malabar Coast, to take on 266 tons of local pepper. Indiamen such as the *Sceptre* carried goods intended for local and regional trade as well as for shipment to England. Its load of pepper would be transferred at Surat to another company vessel arriving from Persia and then departing for England.

As the *Sceptre* sailed from port to port, the crew may have found life aboard ship better than before. After all, their captain knew from personal experience that the common seaman's lot was hard. In the journal he kept during his decades at sea, Barlow recorded all the harsh details. Ordinary seamen were "little better than slaves." Beggars in England generally had "better victuals than we could get"—the dry biscuit and salt beef or pork, boiled in salt water, the wine "as sour as vinegar." Unsuitable food and drink led to the dreaded "bloody flux"—dysentery—which took a steady toll of lives.

AT THE GREAT MOGUL

The East India Company carried home many rare or previously unknown commodities, including a little black bean called coffee. London's first coffeehouse opened its doors in 1652. Hundreds more followed, including ones called the Great Mogul, the Sultaness-Head, and the Floating Coffee House on the Thames, a fashionable establishment built on a barge. Patrons frequented the coffeehouses *(left)* to sip dishes of the beverage as well as China tea, to read newspapers, and to debate issues of the day.

The growing popularity of coffee and coffeehouses provoked a storm of protest from supporters of the English ale industry, who derided the "heathen-ish Liquor" as "base, black, thick, nasty, bitter, stinking, nauseous Puddle-water." Such taunts may have had particular merit in early years, when Arabian beans purchased from Indian merchants in Surat were loaded as ballast on ships, along with black pepper and other pungent bulk goods. By the time they arrived in London, the beans had absorbed the odors around them. To prevent contamination and reduce costs, ships were soon sailing directly to the Red Sea for coffee and returning home without stopping at Indian ports.

Barlow complained about pursers who overcharged the seamen for liquor, tobacco, clothes, and other staples. Wages were poor, he wrote, and the company tried to discourage the lowly sailor's attempts to augment this with a bit of private trade on the side.

What seemed most unjust to Barlow was the arbitrary nature of the East India Company's control. The company could dock a seaman's wages if the cargo was damaged or lost, even if through no fault of the crew. The captain could cane or dismiss a seaman for any breach of discipline. In 1675, long before his remarkable rise to command, Barlow had written: "I wished many times that I had had a trade, so that I might have got my living ashore when I had been weary of the sea."

As the *Sceptre* plied the coastal route, Barlow learned of Kidd's latest adventures. The buccaneer's ship, in its guise as royally commissioned privateer, had been putting into various ports, brazenly demanding to be resupplied with wood and water. In addition, the pirates had seized a small local trader flying English colors, crippled a Portuguese warship that had been sent to intercept them, and raped and pillaged inhabitants of the Laccadive Islands.

Barlow already had departed India when Kidd pulled off his biggest and most fateful coup on January 30, 1698. Off the Malabar Coast he and his men hijacked the *Quedah Merchant* and its rich load of gold as the ship was returning to Surat from Bengal, a northeast region. Once again, Emperor Aurangzeb punished the company for a British pirate's misdeed, suspending trade at Surat and arresting its factors. The company, determined to teach pirates a lesson, pressured the British government into hunting down Kidd. The authorities caught up with him in America in 1699. He was shipped off to London, where he was tried and—despite his protest that "I am the innocentest person of them all"—hanged.

While Kidd was still being hunted, Captain Barlow had brought the *Sceptre* safely

Pirate captain William Kidd *(above)* preyed on ships and ports from Madagascar to India before being captured in 1699 and later sentenced to death. Though he wrote a desperate letter to Parliament pledging to retrieve £100,000 in hidden treasure if pardoned, the government carried out the execution, then encased his body in chains and iron bands and hung it from a gibbet by the Thames *(right)*. The decomposing corpse was meant to serve as a "terror" to would-be pirates.

back home to England in 1698. There his crew unloaded a cargo that included olibanum, or frankincense, a gum resin used by apothecaries; "stickback," used in red sealing wax; and 43 bags of what Barlow referred to as " 'coko-seed,' which is the coffee so much drunk in coffee houses." Barlow was certain that he would be rehired as captain for the next voyage, "for they very well knew

if I had not been in the ship, the owners would have found a far greater charge, and the Company a far greater disappointment in their affairs at Surat." But the owners, who leased the ship to the company, gave the command to another man. Barlow was convinced that he could have had the command if he had had the money to buy it.

Knowing himself far more qualified than his replacement, Barlow refused the offer of a raise in pay to return as chief mate— a wise choice. Due to the new captain's inept handling, the ship was wrecked in the Bristol Channel, and the company's cargo lost. In Barlow's opinion, "It pleased God to answer their expectations according to some of their deserts."

Barlow did take a position as chief mate two more times, but the second of those voyages turned out to be his last. Put out by his captain at the island of St. Helena for insubordination, Barlow received passage aboard a man-of-war headed back to England. Although he had spent a lifetime working on the sea, he returned home that last time in 1703 as a mere ship's passenger.

As the 18th century progressed, the trading rivalry between England and France heated up, escalating during the decline in Moghul power, which began in 1707 with the death of the last great emperor, Aurangzeb. The French established several factories in India, and between 1720 and 1740, their trade there increased tenfold. Then what had begun as a mercantile competition between England and France was transformed into deadly battle when the conflict in Europe spilled onto the subcontinent. The British fired the first shot in 1745, attacking French trading vessels. The French navy retaliated, capturing the prosperous English trading center of Fort St. George at Madras, on India's southeast coast.

Responding to the company's impassioned appeal, in November 1747 the British government sent to India a 24-ship squadron under the command of Admiral Edward Boscawen, with 800

Two men pace the quarterdeck of a Royal Navy ship, a right reserved for officers—and goats, like the one seen lounging next to a poultry cage. To supplement the numerous casks of preserved meat eaten on long voyages, the navy often carried live cattle and seamen sometimes brought their own goats, pigs, chickens, and sheep.

marines and 1,200 soldiers. Those who made up the expedition, which included Irish and Scottish fighters, were heading east for a variety of motives. Many had volunteered for the adventure or to escape a mundane existence. Despite the dangers and hardships at sea, the guarantee of a hot meal and regular pay as well as the promise of a pension provided powerful incentives for the poor. Some may have enlisted for free passage to India, where they promptly jumped ship for a new life. Others were smugglers or debtors pardoned on condition that they enlist. More than a few had been forcibly impressed under the law that allowed government press gangs to pull able-bodied seamen from merchant ships or privateers or pluck them out of local taverns. No one, however, ended up in the

sion for heroism in France, and all but one of her eight brothers and sisters served in the military or were married to soldiers or sailors. Snell's army career ended abruptly, however, when a recruit who had known her as a woman arrived at the regiment. Fearing discovery, she fled—into the Royal Navy. Soon thereafter, she became a member of Boscawen's expedition, headed for India aboard the naval sloop *Swallow.*

Off the coast of Lisbon, Snell found herself fighting for survival. A raging sea whipped the *Swallow* up and down with such force that the mainmast was warping and the rigging ripping away. Standing on a lower deck, Snell and other seamen struggled to keep their footing while raising and lowering the wooden handles of the

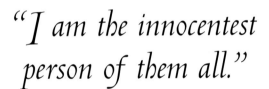

"*I am the innocentest person of them all.*"

navy in quite the way marine James Gray had. He was on the trail of an errant husband.

The husband, Dutch sailor James Summs, belonged to Hannah Snell, a young Worcester woman he had abandoned when she was seven months pregnant. When Snell's child died not long after birth, the grieving mother decided to track Summs down. To find him, she would have to be able to move safely in places a sailor might go. So, donning men's clothing and changing her name to James Gray, 22-year-old Hannah Snell, in November 1745, set out across England on a journey that would carry her far from her home.

Snell's initial travels in England turned up no trace of Summs. Then, surprisingly, she joined the army. Like others, she may have enlisted for monetary reasons—or perhaps it was simply in her blood. Her grandfather had been awarded a battlefield commis-

pumps 40 times a minute to suction water from the damaged hold. It was arduous work, but Snell was quickly learning that life as British marine James Gray was a constant challenge.

Even in calm weather, Snell never got more than four hours to rest, since she and her comrades had to stand watch every four hours. And if she had hoped to leave behind cooking and washing and mending clothing, she was disappointed. Those were her duties as an assistant steward in the officers' mess. Sailors, she discovered, spent most of their days tired and damp. Yet Hannah Snell's greatest trials still lay ahead, in India.

In February 1748 the fleet reached Africa's Cape of Good Hope, where soldiers and marines disembarked to drill for battle. Four months later, they set sail again, arriving in August on India's southeast coast at Fort St. David, the last remaining British trading bastion in the area. Snell found Fort St. David, which overlooked the Bay of Bengal, to be a small stronghold perched on a hill enjoying a clear field of fire that gave way to woods. Three times in the past 19 months the French had attempted to take the fort and failed. During the first assault only, the nawab, or Moghul governor, of the southeast India region called the Carnatic had sent an army, commanded by his son Muhammad Ali, to help the British.

Just outside the fort, prosperous company employees had built houses, their luscious gardens filled with pineapple, pomegranates, and other fruit. A mile to the south lay the associated Indian town of Cuddalore, the whole settlement stretching about three miles along the coast. To the north, across some eight miles of dune and scrub, stood the walled French city of Pondicherry.

Pondicherry was the English expedition's main objective, and on August 8, Snell and her comrades set out to take it. Boscawen, a neophyte in siege warfare, diverted his troops in a protracted siege of a small fort south of Pondicherry. Snell's courage under fire won praise from her officers in the engagement, but the British lost 11 precious days in capturing the place.

The admiral next made the mistake of mounting his siege of Pondicherry itself from the marshy ground northwest of the city. Water filled the trenches as soon as the troops could dig them, and the swamp prevented heavy artillery from being emplaced near the walls. From the sea side, the British ships bombarded the town, but the range was too great, and most rounds fell short. The French, outnumbered nearly two to one, held out within their strong fortifications.

Faced by the intensifying rains of the monsoon period, the British lifted the siege after two months and after more than 1,000 of their own had been killed. Those troops still standing turned back for Fort St. David, trudging down roads deteriorating in the rains and fording dangerously swollen rivers. Ironically, though no one there knew it, in faraway Europe peace negotiators in Aix-la-Chapelle had agreed to end the Indian hostilities before the siege had even begun.

In a hospital in Cuddalore lay the British sick and wounded, transported from Pondicherry by ship. Among them was Hannah Snell. Wading in waist-deep

Painted after her return home, a portrait of Hannah Snell, who disguised herself as a man and enlisted, shows her dressed in martial style. A similar picture graced her 1750 biography, *The Female Soldier*.

During a 1748 siege, French troops defend their fort at Pondicherry *(above)*, where Snell fought until she was wounded in the legs and groin. In July 1750 the *Gentleman's Magazine* wryly praised her exploits and the preservation of her disguise: "Hannah in *breeks* behav'd so well / That none her *softer sex* could tell: / Nor was her *policy* confounded / When near the *mark of nature* wounded / Which proves, what *men* will scarce admit / That *women* are for *secrets* fit."

water in the trenches, she had managed to get off 37 rounds from her musket before falling to enemy fire. British surgeons removed shot from her legs, but she dared not tell them that another piece was embedded in her groin area. She lay in agony, risking her life to hide her true sex. Finally, the pain became so excruciating that she decided to extract the metal herself, aided by a female Indian nurse who brought her salves and cotton to dress the wound.

By the time Snell recovered, the *Swallow* had sailed, and she was assigned to the *Eltham*. In Madeira the ship's captain impressed seamen from a privateer. Snell found the men "in the greatest affliction, for being forced from them they loved." Sailing with the navy meant a much longer tour of duty and more time away from their families than they had intended. Touched by a loyalty so different from that shown by her husband, Snell did what she could to ease their lives, smuggling liquor for them through her post in the officers' mess.

When the ship stopped in Lisbon, Snell went ashore. Drinking wine at a tavern, she encountered a talkative Englishman from a Dutch ship. He had just returned from Genoa, he told her, where a Dutchman named James Summs had been executed for stabbing to death a local resident. When he had seen Summs before his death, the stranger confided, the condemned man had begged forgiveness of the wife he had wronged. Stunned, Snell made her way back to her ship.

Back in London in June 1750, her quest over and her military service completed, Snell collected her wages and the two suits of clothing due from her regiment, which she promptly sold. Then she joined a group of marines from the *Eltham* for a final drink. She told all, knowing they could later attest to the truth of her adventures. When they

COUNT ROUPEE. _Vide Hyde Park._

"Count Roupee" gallops through London's Hyde Park in this 18th-century lampoon of nabobs—as company employees grown rich in India were known. The stereotypical nabob lived in an ostentatious mansion, rode in a garish carriage, and bought his way into the peerage and into Parliament. Although only a few dozen nabobs fit this description, the actions of some engendered a general dislike in England for all of them.

recovered from their shock, her mates applauded her courage. One even proposed marriage, but Snell refused. She resolved, her biographer wrote, "never to engage with any Man living."

In fact, Hannah Snell would marry again, twice. Before that, her exploits were celebrated in print, and she went onstage in her regimentals to perform military drills. Snell then opened a public house in London called the Female Warrior, which proved to be highly prosperous.

Not all of Hannah Snell's fellow veterans at Pondicherry had come to India with Boscawen's expedition. Many had traveled there to work for the East India Company factories. Some had gone voluntarily; others had been shipped off by families eager to

rid themselves of problem sons. If they did not improve in India, at least they would be less of an embarrassment there. In fact, a number of these young men would thrive. The shrinking of the Moghul emperor's influence during the 18th century, regional disputes for leadership among some Indian rulers, and the fight between the British and the French for supremacy would create unparalleled opportunities. Those who made the most of them could become rich and powerful beyond their wildest imaginings, earning themselves a uniquely Indian title: nabob.

The eldest son of a Shropshire country squire and lawyer, Robert Clive had been in trouble as a boy and was described by his uncle as "out of measure addicted" to fighting. Young Clive had even formed a gang of youths to extort money from shopkeepers who did not want their windows broken. His father sent him at age 14 to a school in England's southeast borough of Hemel Hempstead to learn penmanship and accounting. Those would be useful skills for someone being shipped to India to work for the East India Company.

In the summer of 1744, Clive's ship dropped anchor at Madras, where he would become a company writer, or copy clerk. Across the yellow sand, the 18-year-old Clive could see the fortified walls of the company factory, Fort St. George, as well as the housetops and church spire rising above them. Beneath the hot June sun, all shone a brilliant white, like polished marble, an effect caused by the burnt seashell cement that covered the walls.

To the right, or north side, of the fort, beyond

For Clive such wonders paled beside the tedium of being on the lowest rung of the company's civil service career ladder. The monotony of recording bales of textiles and copying invoices heightened the bouts of severe depression that would afflict him throughout his life. Twice in those first years he attempted suicide, but the gun misfired. "It seems," he said, "that fate must be reserving me for some purpose."

That purpose began to reveal itself in 1746, when hostilities with the French broke out and the enemy captured Madras. Disguising himself as an Indian, Clive escaped and made his way south to Fort St. David, which he then helped to defend. Deemed as "being of a Martial disposition," he was commissioned an ensign, the lowest junior officer. In 1748 he distinguished himself during the siege of

"Fate must be reserving me for some purpose."

a marsh, Clive would find the narrow, crowded streets and bustling bazaars of Black Town, as the Indian section of the city was known. Indians, Armenians, and other non-Europeans lived and traded there. The scents of incense, jasmine, and ripe fruit mingled with the aroma of spicy food and burning dung, used as fuel for cooking.

Most of the British resided within Fort St. George or to its south. The wealthiest merchants had built weekend retreats in the classical style farther inland, to the west. Westward, the coastal sands gave way to paddy fields, irrigation pools, and temple towns. Littering this landscape were towering palms and banyan trees, which impressed sightseers with "branches [that] bend down to the ground, take root and thence spring out anew; thus forming innumerable arches."

Pondicherry, holding his position against a heavy French assault.

After Madras was restored to the British under the peace treaty, Clive was appointed commissary in charge of provisioning the troops, a financially profitable post. It also provided him with priceless experience in management and logistics. As he purchased food from merchants and found bulls, camels, and elephants to haul the guns and stores, he learned how to deal with Indians and win their trust, an essential skill for the future. For despite the Aix-la-Chapelle treaty, the British and French had begun a new war, with new tactics.

The commercial rivals had embarked on a campaign of indirect warfare. As the Moghul emperor's authority declined, the two European trading companies sought more and more to meddle in local affairs in order to secure trade. Each backed different

Wonders of the Nabobs

Ambitious employees of the East India Company would acquire not only money and power during their Indian tenure but rich and valuable artifacts as well. Once home in England, the nabobs could proudly display these sumptuous pieces, which reflected their owners' wealth and evoked life on the subcontinent for people who had never journeyed there. One of the greatest such collections would be amassed by Robert Clive.

In India, gift giving, as a display of one's wealth and as an expression of hospitality, permeated the culture. Since Clive's military and diplomatic activities brought him into repeated contact with Indian rulers, he may have obtained part of his collection at the royal receptions known as durbars. Ornately decorated and bejeweled daggers like those owned by Clive were frequently given as durbar gifts. Such weapons were mainly ceremonial pieces, traditionally worn under a sash at the waist.

During Clive's time in India, the English often emulated Indian customs in their own homes. When entertaining guests, Clive may have used his silver durbar set *(bottom right)* in an Indian tradition involving the chewing of *pan* to aid digestion. The ingredients for pan, a slightly intoxicating mixture of nuts and spices wrapped in a betel leaf, were placed in small ornate boxes set on trays. Servants used the tall-necked vessels of the durbar set to sprinkle guests with aromatic rose water, which was also kept in the set's little perfume stands. When a host served his guests pan, reported an Englishman, it was an indication that the visit was coming to a close and the guests would soon take their leave.

As with the durbar set, Clive probably acquired his collection of hookahs—water pipes that were used for smoking tobacco—as well as the beautifully embroidered hookah furnishings for his personal use. Although Europeans were initially reluctant to take up smoking tobacco with water pipes, hookahs had become very popular by Clive's time, and at least one attendant, who was referred to as a hookah burdar, would be hired to attend to the equipment itself.

This gleaming silver-and-gilt durbar set decorated in a teardrop pattern and this ceremonial dagger with a gilded and ruby-studded white-jade handle are part of Robert Clive's magnificent collection, gathered during his years in India.

This bejeweled and enameled hookah and the rich cloth for covering its stem belonged to Clive. A portrait of another 18th-century Englishman, doctor and Calcutta mayor William Fullerton, shows him lounging on a carpet smoking a hookah *(left).* Pieces of a durbar set stand along the carpet's edge; dagger handles can be seen in the waist sashes of two of the Indians.

Smoking was an expensive habit, due to the high price of tobacco. But some people, claimed British lawyer William Hickey, "would much rather be deprived of their dinner than their hookah."

Other items in Clive's collection included European-style furniture manufactured by Indians. Around the turn of the 18th century, artisans in the coastal town of Vizagapatam (situated between Calcutta and Madras) responded to European tastes by crafting beautiful ivory-inlaid and veneered cabinets, desks, and tables. Clive accumulated ivory chess sets, painted-ivory playing cards, ornate boxes, textiles, and fly whisks. Not surprisingly, Clive, who would become a British military hero, had also acquired a vast array of war booty—shields, swords, daggers, matchlocks, and elephant equipment.

Clive housed his treasures at Claremont, his home in Surrey, England. His son Edward and daughter-in-law Henrietta Herbert added to the collection after they went to India in 1798, where Edward served as governor of Madras. They contributed several items that had belonged to Indian ruler Tipu Sultan.

In collecting and displaying artifacts amassed during their time abroad, the Clives were following English tradition. But not all of the English were impressed by such acquisitions. After being "obliged to admire" his host's Indian artifacts, one man pleaded, "Defend me I say from a Nabobs collection."

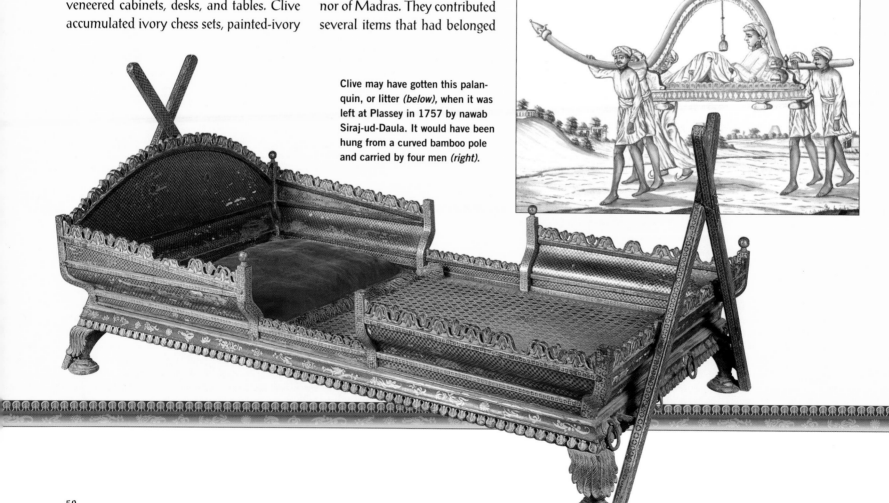

Clive may have gotten this palanquin, or litter *(below)*, when it was left at Plassey in 1757 by nawab Siraj-ud-Daula. It would have been hung from a curved bamboo pole and carried by four men *(right)*.

This ornate rosewood chest inlaid with ivory served as a writing desk and as a dressing table with mirror. It was produced by Vizagapatam artisans.

claimants to the thrones, supporting them with arms, sepoys (Indian troops commanded by Europeans), and European troops.

In July 1751, Clive, recently made a captain, led a small supply expedition to Trichinopoly, some 200 miles southwest of Madras. A great rock fortress, it was the last redoubt of Muhammad Ali, who had once helped the British hold Fort St. David. In the dispute over the throne of the Carnatic—the princely state encompassing the coastal cities of Madras, Cuddalore, and Pondicherry—the British had chosen to back Ali, whose father had been the nawab until he was killed by the forces of the French-backed claimant, Chanda Sahib. These French-supported forces were the same ones that were now besieging Trichinopoly.

When Clive arrived with provisions, Muhammad Ali told the young officer that a raid on Arcot, where Chanda Sahib had installed himself, might divert the enemy and relieve the pressure on Trichinopoly. By the time Clive returned to Madras, the British governor there had already decided to execute this plan, and Clive persuaded the governor to let him lead it.

On September 6, 1751, a ragtag-looking column of warriors straggled out of Madras under Clive's command. The 300 sepoys wore only ordinary native shirts above bare legs that stirred up orange-tinted dust to the beat of the tom-tom. As for the 200 or so European soldiers, their red uniforms could not conceal their lack of training, discipline, or experienced leadership. They were for the most part ruffians and misfits who had come to India because they could not make it at home. Of the eight officers who led them, half were former company civilian employees.

Under Clive's surprisingly resourceful command, his force demonstrated remarkable discipline. Their destination, Arcot, was some 60 miles inland. The troops kept going, through blistering heat and a raging rainstorm that turned the dust to mud. Six days after setting out, they approached Arcot's gates to make an astonishing discovery: The garrison of 1,100 Indians left to defend the city had disappeared. The English later claimed that the defenders, having heard reports of how the English-led column had marched right through the rainstorm with its powerful omens of thunder and lightning, had decided it would be useless to resist such a foe. More likely, the approach of a force of uncertain numbers caused them to temporarily abandon Arcot to await additional troops, since they had only retreated to an encampment not far from the city.

To retain a veil of political legitimacy, Clive claimed the fort not for the British but for Muhammad Ali. Then he settled in to wait. Within two weeks, the enemy camp had grown to 3,000 men. In the dead of night, Clive led his 500 troops in a daring attack that broke up the camp and caused the enemy to flee. Soon, Chanda Sahib followed the script that Muhammad Ali had envisioned. He withdrew 4,000 of his troops and 150 French soldiers from the siege of Trichinopoly and sent them to recapture Arcot.

Clive had thus accomplished his mission of relieving pressure on Muhammad Ali. A more experienced soldier almost certainly would have abandoned Arcot at this point and returned to Madras. But hungry for glory, Clive stayed on. He and his force holed up in the fort inside the city while the nawab's men laid siege from the surrounding streets and houses. Though battle, disease, and exhaustion thinned their ranks by more than one-third, Clive's soldiers responded to their commander's courage and resolute leadership, holding out for a total of 50 grueling days.

Then, in November, the enemy attempted to storm the fort. To batter down the high wooden gates, they drove ahead of them elephants with iron fixed in their foreheads. But the huge beasts, stung by a fusillade of bullets from the fort, turned and stampeded, trampling to death hundreds of the attackers. They pulled back after an hour's fight and withdrew for good the following day upon news that formidable relief columns were en route to aid Clive: British from Madras and 6,000 Marathas (Indians from the region south of Bombay) hired by Muhammad Ali.

Clive's audacious victory at Arcot turned the tide against Chanda Sahib and the French. He went on to help break the siege at Trichinopoly, foiling the French threat to dominate trade in the Carnatic. In 1752 Muhammad Ali ascended his father's old throne. The grateful new nawab gave substantial grants of land to the company. And upon his unlikely young deliverer, Clive, the new ruler bestowed the name Steady in War, observing, "I am well assured that fortune is bent in your favour."

But fortune proved fickle. In 1753, the 28-year-old hero returned to England and attempted to establish a lifestyle as extrav-

Wearing jewels and a gold-trimmed gown and grasping a great sword, Muhammad Ali, nawab of the Carnatic, poses for a portrait around 1774 *(right)*. Some 25 years before, he and a small garrison had tenaciously held the sprawling rock fortress of Trichinopoly in the southern Carnatic *(below)* against the superior forces of a French-backed rival for the region's throne.

53

agant as the diamond-studded sword awarded him by the company. He mounted an expensive campaign for a seat in the House of Commons and lost. The modest fortune he had accumulated as a commissary soon shrank. With the threat of another war with France looming, he accepted a commission in the Royal Army as a lieutenant colonel and leaped at the company's offer to be governor of Fort St. David.

By the time he arrived back in India in 1756, however, the company's military priorities focused not on the French but on the wealthy province of Bengal, the fastest-growing trade center in India. The company had established a thriving factory there in Fort William, and some 100,000 Indians had settled outside the walls of the fort to create the city of Calcutta. By spring 1756 the newly enthroned nawab of Bengal, Siraj-ud-Daula, had become anxious about the burgeoning European presence and increasing preparations for war by the French and the British. Worried for his region's peace, the 27-year-old ruler demanded that the British and French demolish the new fortifications in Calcutta and the French settlement at Chandernagore, some 25 miles to the north. The French sent a mollifying response, claiming they were only making repairs from storm damage, but the British refused the demands outright, insulting the princely envoy in the process. Learning of the British response, an angry Siraj-ud-Daula exclaimed, "What honour is left to us,

when a few traders who have not yet learned to wash their bottoms reply to the ruler's order by expelling his envoy?"

The nawab took action in June 1756. After four days' severe fighting, his troops seized Calcutta and Fort William. For the British, who had been confident of their ability to fend off any attacking Bengali force, Calcutta's loss was a heavy blow. The nawab's occupation also resulted in an inadvertent atrocity that would enflame British sentiment against the Indians.

On the night of June 20, when the fort fell, the nawab ordered the imprisonment of a number of company employees. The captors locked their prisoners in a room inside Fort William that had served the British as a jail. Known as the Black Hole (the name for all detention cells in military barracks), it was small—about 18 feet by 15 feet—and situated partially underground,

While residents stroll on the green around Fort William *(background)* and St. Anne's Church *(foreground)*, an early-18th-century governor of Calcutta sets out on an official duty preceded by flag bearers and mounted bodyguards *(far right)*.

On June 20, 1756, British prisoners in Calcutta's Black Hole clamber over the dead to reach water passed through the windows by guards. The only woman thrown into the cramped prison after the fall of Fort William was Mary Carey, who had been refused passage on British vessels evacuating women and children because she was part Indian. She survived the ordeal.

with scarce light and ventilation provided by a couple of tiny barred windows. Crammed into the Black Hole on one of the hottest and most humid nights of the year, employees slowly suffocated. The nawab slept on, unaware of their plight because guards hesitated to wake him for instructions. When the prison door was finally opened the next morning, many of the British lay dead. One who survived penned a grisly—and embellished—account of the tragedy that gave enduring notoriety to the Black Hole of Calcutta.

To re-claim Calcutta, the company turned to Robert Clive. Clive accepted leadership of an expedition, knowing victory could assure his future. "This expedition," he confided to his father, "if attended with success may enable me to do great things." Backed by five warships from the Royal Navy, his 2,000 British and Indian troops quickly routed the nawab's forces. Clive signed a peace agreement with Siraj-ud-Daula in February 1757, then found a way to get rid of the young ruler.

That spring Clive entered into a conspiracy with an influential ring of Indians in Bengal—the Jagat Seths, a powerful family who acted as bankers to the nawab, and Mir Jafar, the nawab's great-uncle, one of his top military commanders, and an eager aspirant for his throne. To keep Siraj-ud-Daula from getting suspicious, Clive sent letters proclaiming, "I desire nothing so much as to live in peace and friendship with you."

The nawab remained distrustful, but in the end he could not stop the conspirators. On June 23, 1757, the British force faced his army at Plassey, some 95 miles north of Calcutta. Clive had about 3,000 troops, the nawab 50,000. But numbers were meaningless. Most of the nawab's men had been bought off in advance through Mir Jafar, and a British victory required only an artillery bombardment and a strong infantry assault. The conspirators then hunted down and killed the young nawab. A few days later, Clive saw Mir Jafar installed as the new ruler of Bengal and two neighboring provinces, Bihar and Orissa.

Then came the payoff. Mir Jafar restored British trading privileges and excluded the French from Bengal. Moreover, he assigned enough land to the company so that the tax-

After the Battle of Plassey in 1757, a triumphant Robert Clive stands beneath a British flag to greet co-conspirator Mir Jafar, who betrayed the nawab of Bengal to gain the throne. While the nawab's forces included elephants adorned with scarlet embroidered cloth, earlier Moghul rulers provided their military elephants with armor. The early-17th-century elephant armor at right was brought back to England by Clive's son and daughter-in-law.

es would pay its growing army and subsidize the war against the French down in the Madras region. For the destruction at Calcutta, the nawab agreed to pay war restitution. Company employees also benefited handsomely, as money was lavished upon soldiers, officers, and senior officials.

Clive, the newly appointed company governor for Bengal, reaped the richest harvest. He received enormous monetary presents from Mir Jafar, enriching him beyond his wildest dreams. Then named to a high military rank in the nawab's own army, Clive applied to the court for a *jagir*—a grant of revenue-producing land that customarily went with such rank. The jagir produced a substantial amount of annual revenue. It represented, Clive wrote, "my future power, my future grandeur."

When he returned to England in 1761, 36-year-old Clive was one of the richest men in the country, one of the first of the nabobs. The Bengali pronunciation of the Indian title *nawab*, nabob was applied to those, like Clive, who returned from India with great wealth and tried to buy their way into English society. This time Clive had enough to purchase a seat in the House of Commons.

Back in Bengal, the East India Company's public and private greed was leading to a collapse of the political structure. The company's senior civil servants and army officers not only exacted generous "presents" and outright bribes from the new nawab and lesser officials but profited enormously from private trade as well. East India Company employees had always engaged in business on the side to supplement their notoriously low salaries, but the events in 1757 set off an explosive expansion of activity.

The employees extended personal enterprises into parts of the Indian provinces where Europeans had never traded before, dealing in commodities whose customs duties were important revenue sources for the nawab. The company long had enjoyed the right to trade in Bengal without payment of customs, using a special *dastak,* or pass, granted by the nawab. Without the Indian ruler's consent, the British had been

routinely extending this privilege to their personal trade. And to further bolster their burgeoning incomes, some employees brazenly had sold the dastak to Indian merchants. Senior employees were building up such huge nest eggs that they could retire after only a dozen years' service in Bengal, returning home as youthful and wealthy nabobs.

When the nawab Mir Jafar balked at British demands for ever-more revenue, company troops surrounded his palace and forced him to abdicate in favor of his son-in-law, Mir Kasim. The new nawab paid the British their asking price for helping him take the throne, ceding three of his most important districts, a third of his land revenues. But Mir Kasim, too, soon realized that private inland trade expansion and continuing monetary demands by the British were draining his coffers. To make matters worse, local agents working for the British were terrorizing the countryside, forcing merchants and shopkeepers to trade at unfair prices. Mir Kasim took up arms against the company in 1763.

Clive, of all people, had been appalled by the actions of the company officials when news filtered back to England. "Corruption, Licentiousness, and Want of Principle seem to have possessed the minds of all the Civil Servants," he wrote. In London, the company directors sent orders to India that prohibited duty-free private inland trade and barred the taking of presents from the nawab. And Clive was asked to go back to Bengal as governor to crack down on abuses in private trade and restore order. He agreed.

While the directors made plans, the company's army drove Mir Kasim from his throne. He appealed for aid to the nawab of the neighboring province of Oudh and his guest, Emperor Shah Alam II, who was attempting to unite remnants of the old Moghul domain. In 1764 their makeshift alliance met the British at Buxar, some 400 miles northwest of Calcutta. Once again the British prevailed.

Clive received the

Beneath a canopy in a great hall, Moghul emperor Shah Alam II grants Robert Clive the diwani—or tax-collecting and civil-administration power—for Bengal, setting the stage for the British Raj. The painting is fanciful; the real 1765 event took place in the Englishman's tent.

news while his ship was anchored off Madras in April 1765 and immediately dashed off a letter to London. The British victory at Buxar had put him in a position to dictate terms to the new nawab and to the emperor himself. "We must indeed become the Nabobs ourselves in Fact, if not in Name, perhaps totally without Disguise," Clive declared. In order to achieve this, he concluded a peace treaty at Allahabad in northern India on August 12, 1765. The site of their historic parley was Clive's own tent, where he improvised a throne for Shah Alam II by placing a draped armchair on the dining table. The makeshift setting was appropriate, since the emperor's authority now amounted to little more than window dressing.

Under the Treaty of Allahabad, the emperor turned over to the company the vital function of his diwan, or revenue collector, for Bengal, Bihar, and Orissa. The East India Company would keep all the tax revenues yielded by these three rich provinces. The emperor in return would be given a large annual stipend to support himself and the imperial household. The company would also undertake the defense of these provinces and the financing of their newest nawab, who would now be truly a figurehead.

Thanks largely to the military prowess and clever intrigues of Robert Clive, the businessmen of the East India Company were now the de facto rulers of a sizable and strategically important area of the subcontinent. In only a century and a half, the company had transformed itself from a seaborne trading concern petitioning the Moghul emperor for favors to a land-based powerbroker deciding who would or would not rule parts of the subcontinent. After Mir Kasim and Shah Alam II's defeat, Robert Clive claimed, "It is scarcely a Hyperbole to say that the whole Moghul Empire is in our hands." He may have been premature. But there is no doubt that this former juvenile delinquent and clerk, who after many attempts during his life finally killed himself at age 49, had brought about the beginning of the fabled British Raj.

Building an Army in British India

As the East India Company gained a political foothold in peninsular India in the mid-1700s and the economic stakes increased, it became necessary to create a permanent army to defend and expand its interests. Company officials, faced with a demand for soldiers that exceeded the supply, turned to the soldiers of their Indian allies to augment their troops.

The Hindu and Muslim soldiers, called sepoys (from the Persian word *sipahi*, meaning horseman or soldier), were formed into companies, and British officers armed and trained the men in the manner of European troops. Major Stringer Lawrence, often called the father of the Indian army, raised the first native regiments in Madras in 1748; Robert Clive, commander of the army at the Battle of Plassey in 1757, was the first to organize the Bengal companies into battalions. By the time of the British victory at Seringapatam in 1799, native battalions were a valued and visible presence alongside the company's European and British troops.

The company's permanent army continued to grow, and by the mid-19th century it was the largest and most diverse military force in Asia—and its numbers were dominated by native soldiers. Without them, it is unlikely that the British could have built and maintained their empire.

East India Company forces make their final assault on the fortress of Seringapatam, where in just one hour on May 4, 1799, they crushed the Mysore empire. Their effectiveness was a credit to Stringer Lawrence, shown here in a portrait from about 1775: As the army's first commander in chief, he organized their training.

The Coming of the Cavalry

Members of the cavalry regiment Skinner's Horse—known as Yellow Boys for the color of their coats—practice fending off a cavalry charge in this painting from about 1840 *(left)*. Astride their agile horses, these irregular cavalry units could easily outmaneuver and fatigue a force on foot. Colonel James Skinner *(below)* founded the elite cavalry unit that helped prove the value of mounted soldiers in the company's army.

From their first campaigns for Indian territory, the British had relied almost solely on foot soldiers. It was the infantry who won battles, they believed; cavalry units were expensive and undisciplined. But commanders of the various armies in the field disagreed, pointing out how successfully Indian enemy forces had used their cavalry against them. The East India Company soon saw the wisdom in this.

Relying initially on mounted contingents provided by Indian allies, the company set about raising irregular cavalry units that were eventually inducted into permanent army service. The first irregular regiment to be formally accepted into the company's Bengal Army was that of James Skinner in 1803. Once allied with French and Indian forces fighting against the British, Skinner and many of his men took up the company's cause and colors when his forces were defeated.

Though treated by some as an outcast due to his mixed-race heritage—he was the son of a Scottish captain in the East India Company and a Rajput princess—Skinner proved himself an accomplished soldier and a skilled negotiator. He and the soldiers under his command formed the company regiment known as Skinner's Horse, which earned respect and distinction in many campaigns.

Soon, quality horses and skilled horsemen were in great demand. Company scouts began to follow horse fairs and track horse-trading activity, and Arab stallions were imported from Europe, the Middle East, and Africa for new breeding farms. Skinner and other cavalry officers recruited their soldiers from groups of skilled peasant warriors and from elite Hindu and Muslim military families who had served the Moghul empire and other Indian rulers. The yellow of their uniforms was also the battle color of the Rajput princes and was perhaps chosen by Skinner to honor not only his own ancestors but also those of his men.

A Common Bond of Honor

In 1835 a native battalion of Rajputs led a successful British assault at Bharatpur. Their victory was all the sweeter because, 30 years before, their fathers had charged into virtually the same battle, but with a very different outcome: In 1805 the battalion was roundly defeated and their colors shredded in the bloody assault. By tradition, the tattered flag should have been destroyed and a new one dedicated, but the colors mysteriously disappeared. When they next appeared, the faded fragments had been tied to the flag that was raised in victory at Bharatpur.

Unbeknown to their British officers, men of the defeated regiment had cut the remnants of their colors into strips, and secretly handed them down from father to son. Now, 30 years later, the disappointment and dishonor felt so keenly by the soldiers for so many years was replaced by an overwhelming pride.

It was this high regard for glory, honor, and the military profession that created a bond of trust and admiration between British and Indian soldiers. While Indian sepoys knew that they would never receive the professional respect accorded British and European soldiers, they remained for the most part faithful to their officers and loyal to the company that provided their livelihood.

At an elaborate regimental durbar, cavalry commander Colonel James Skinner *(center, rear)* and his son prepare to receive a soldier seeking to join Skinner's Horse. Members of the cavalry regiment, wearing ceremonial red jackets over their yellow uniforms, kneel at the sides of the carpeted pavilion.

A Brahman garlands the flags of the 35th Bengal Light Infantry at a presentation of colors ceremony, depicted in this watercolor from about 1845. Honoring the tools of one's craft or calling once a year was a Hindu tradition.

CHAPTER TWO

Making a Life on the Subcontinent

In a British home in Calcutta, a memsahib, or European mistress of a household, examines a new hat from an Indian tailor as her English butler looks on and Indian servants perform various duties. As Britons began coming to the subcontinent with their families, they developed a lifestyle neither wholly British nor wholly Indian, but a distinct combination known as Anglo-Indian.

 ix oars cut the water smoothly as Indian boatmen sent their shallow-draft vessel and its passengers up the Hooghly River on November 3, 1777. Twenty-eight-year-old William Hickey could find no comfortable perch in the boat, known as a panchway, which had a low-roofed shelter for protection from the sun and rain but no seats. Hickey and his fellow travelers were forced to sit cross-legged on a platform as miles of green jungle, broken only by tiny mud-hut villages, passed. Discomfort was soon forgotten, however, as the river took a turn to the east and a breathtaking stretch of land sprang into view. Hickey was enthralled. "The verdure throughout on every side was beautiful beyond imagination, the whole of the landscape being more luxuriant than I had any expectation of seeing in the burning climate of Bengal." This was Garden Reach, entryway to the most prosperous and booming city in all of British India: Calcutta.

Hickey expected to make his life and fortune in Calcutta, where a network of professional, family, and school connections—not to mention his own considerable charm—ensured a welcome. As a lawyer, he would find plenty of work. After all, England had just established the Supreme Court here, put in place, as the British saw it, to "protect natives from oppression and to give India the benefit of English law." With these factors in mind, Hickey had high hopes of making this trip more rewarding than his first sojourn in India nearly a decade before.

William Hickey, born in 1749, had proved a disappointment as a young man to his father, successful London lawyer Joseph Hickey. Joseph had given his youngest son a good education and trained him in the family law firm, but William insisted on keeping bad company. When his son juggled the firm's books and stole money for drink and fashionable courtesans, a distressed Joseph Hickey saw no other course than to send 19-year-old William to Madras, India, to become an East India Company military cadet. Finding the pay abysmal, William soon came home to work in his father's firm again. Now India beckoned once more, this time promising far different prospects for a young lawyer than it had for a cadet.

The elegant mansions of Garden Reach were surrounded by groves and lawns that ran down to the river. The houses belonged to high-ranking East India Company employees and their families, who frequently abandoned the city for the reach's cooler and more refreshing air. Hickey's host for his first months in Calcutta owned a home here, and this is where the young Englishman disembarked. Ascending a 30-foot bank, he paused to look farther up the river and caught his first glimpse of "the magnificent city of Calcutta."

Rebuilt by the British after its 1756 capture by the nawab of Bengal, the grand city of Calcutta appeared on the right-hand bank

PASSAGE TO INDIA

Until the advent of the steamship in the late 1820s, traveling from England to India was a grueling voyage of six months or more. Affluent travelers paid for roundhouse cabins with portholes, located just under the stern's upper, or poop, deck, while less-expensive cabins were found below. People with very little money rode in steerage, condemned as "worse than a dog-kennel" by one traveler. An open compartment, steerage lacked privacy, fresh air, and light.

Seasickness abounded, but tedium and close proximity also exacted a toll. Arguments broke out, some over the favors of single women. To prevent "imprudent attachments" and protect reputations, unmarried women were usually chaperoned.

Traveling the final distance from ship to shore sometimes proved its own trial. In Madras dangerous breakers kept ships from close anchorage, so boatmen rowed out to ferry passengers through the waves and carried women the final yards to dry land (above).

style, square houses with splendid porticoes, verandas, and arcades on the first floor and tall verandas, columned and pedimented, on the second. Above were flat, balustraded roofs, ornamented with urns. In houses of this scale, drawing rooms 80 feet long and 40 feet high and wide were not unusual.

Calcutta's public buildings were classically splendid, too. On Esplanade Row stood Government House, where Hickey was to meet British India's first governor general, Warren Hastings, and Council House. Intersecting the row was Court House Street, which stretched north to Tank Square, with its great, embanked pool supplying drinking water to the city. Bordering the square were the Court House, where the Supreme Court met and Hickey would soon be practicing, and on the river side, the partially destroyed old Fort William. The riverbank by the old fort, where the warehouses were, was crowded with European merchants' cargo. In the water below the Old Fort Ghat—as the ramp leading into the river was called—among flocks of pleasure boats and tall-masted ships, Hindu men bathed in their dhotis, or loincloths, and women in their saris. Nearby was the Holwell monument, commemorating the victims of the 1756 Black Hole disaster.

Calcutta's multiethnic population resided primarily in three different sections of the city. The White Town, where the British lived, stretched south from Tank Square; an intermediate area, where Armenians, Jews, Arabs, Parsis, and Euro-Asians could be found, lay immediately north of the square; and the Black Town, located still farther to the north, was home to the Indians, predominantly Hindus. The subtowns were not sharply delineated, however. Little huts for Indian servants surrounded the compounds of the great houses, and bazaars crept up to the walls of official buildings. One irritated visitor thought everything looked jumbled, "as if all the houses had been thrown up in the air, and falled down again by accident."

The disorder was a sign of the enormous vitality of mercantile British India. British residents in European fashions, sepoys in

as visitors traveled upriver, heralded by the looming mass of the new Fort William, an octagon with seven gates. Set in a huge clearing, the fort was separated from the town by a half-mile green called the esplanade. Along the bordering streets, Esplanade Row and Chowringhee Road, rose the great white houses that earned Calcutta the name City of Palaces.

The buildings seemed palaces indeed to Hickey and other new arrivals—bigger than the London houses of the aristocracy and as big as the palaces of Venice. The British merchants liked magnificence. They built their homes in the approved neoclassic turbans and red coats, hundreds of servants in white, and many more filled Calcutta, riding the crest of the city's rise. Carriages, palanquins, and carts jostled for space in streets thronged with animals—horses, dogs, cows, and brightly dressed camels and elephants. Business was conducted outdoors as well, by Indian peddlers, letter writers, barbers, and such. If it all seemed a jumble to some people, it suited William Hickey just fine.

For the better part of three decades, between 1777 and 1807, William Hickey would live handsomely in Calcutta, floating through the city's tensions and intrigues, observing it all and having a fine time. Later, in comfortable, and rather bored, retirement in Buckinghamshire, he would remember every moment and write it all down. His description of proper British society in Calcutta was liberally laced with frank accounts of his own often drunken, though rarely meanspirited, behavior.

Other Britons who wrote extensively of their experiences provided somewhat different perspectives of life on the subcontinent. Over the years, as British rule spread and solidified, India attracted people who tended to be less libertine and more respectable and bourgeois. They did not come, like William Hickey, to have a good time and make a pile of money in the cities. A privileged few came as diplomats in the courts of dependent princes and as official "residents"—company representatives controlling business in remote areas. The majority came to work as civil servants and administrators and to serve as soldiers at far-flung military posts.

One, a British army officer's wife and famed children's author, Mary Martha Sherwood, would write of life on these military posts and the awful plight of many of the children she met there—whether European, "half-caste" (of Indian and European parentage), or Indian. A different sort of company wife, inveterate traveler and romantic Fanny Parks, would write of India's people, ceremonies, and traditions. And so, in his or her own way,

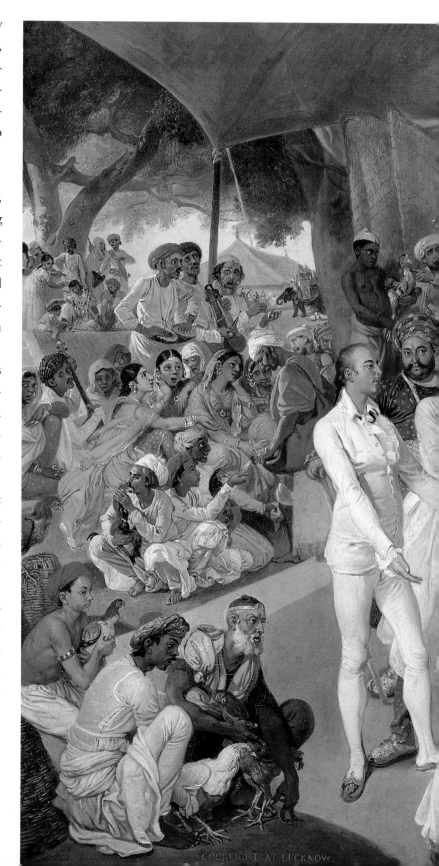

Stripped down to his white waistcoat, Colonel John Mordaunt talks with the nawab of Oudh *(center)* during a cockfight. Around the two men, Indian merchants, soldiers, musicians, and dancers mingle with European guests. Mordaunt, who commanded the nawab's bodyguard in the late 18th century, was one of the many Britons attracted to India.

Hickey, Sherwood, and Parks each embraced India and, as they put their experiences down on paper, created vivid, yet varyied, pictures of life on the subcontinent.

In the first year and a half after his arrival in Calcutta, William Hickey underwent a transformation. Though he continued to indulge himself, he changed from a dissolute young man about town into a respected and prosperous lawyer. It was with some pride that he noted his changed ways. "Notwithstanding I lived so dissipated a life in point of drinking and late hours, no man labored harder," he would write. "I was always at my desk before seven in the morning, and, with the break of half an hour for breakfast, never ceased work until dinner; after which, unless upon emergencies, I never took pen in hand. I had sufficient business to occupy myself and three native clerks." All he lacked was the proper companion. He found her during a trip back to England in the early 1780s.

Stylish, pretty, and sweet-natured, Charlotte Barry was a London courtesan. Hickey and Barry fell in love while she was living with another man. This lover reacted violently to Barry's decision to leave him, seizing a knife and threatening to "bury it in her heart." Hickey grabbed a fire poker and stepped between the raging man and his intended victim. Barry then showed her own courage, sending Hickey away in order to defuse the situation. The following day, Hickey returned, whisked Barry away in his carriage, and asked her to marry him. Fearing he might regret binding himself to her, Barry turned down his proposal but agreed to take his name. "From that hour," he wrote, "I considered myself as much her husband as the strictest forms and ceremonies of the Church could have made me." On June 30, 1783, they arrived

INDIA'S CASTE SYSTEM

The Hindu caste system had its origins in a sacred hymn dividing society into four levels, or *varnas*, which came to be determined by birth. On top were Brahmans *(left)*, priests, teachers, and scholars. Warriors, called *kshatriyas*, came next, then the farmer and merchant *vaishyas*. At bottom were *shudras*, who were to serve the upper castes. Untouchables fell outside the caste system and were consigned to tasks deemed too polluting for others.

The system influenced the lives of many Hindus. Religious sanctions, for example, forbade marrying outside one's caste. Eating food made by members of lower castes was thought defiling. And as a rule, members of different castes could not engage in professions reserved for others. Violating such taboos could result in the severest of punishments—expulsion from one's caste.

in Calcutta, for all intents and purposes a married couple.

There were certain practical rituals for Britons in India, as William Hickey had discovered when he first arrived and as Charlotte would soon learn. Perhaps foremost was the choice of a *banian,* a corruption of a word meaning "merchant." A banian handled all one's affairs, from setting up a household to arranging loans, taking a commission on every transaction. This type of Indian businessman was essential to the British who, in general, did not bother to learn enough Bengali, the local language, or Persian, the administrative language, to conduct business. Besides, few Britons understood the complicated nature of local business.

Banians were responsible for hiring servants, of which a staggering number were required, partly because of the occupational restrictions imposed by the Hindu class structure, known as the caste system, and partly for prestige. The British had to learn that the *kansamah,* or butler, who controlled the entire household, could shop for food but not carry it home; that the cook did not wash up; that Hindus in Calcutta could have nothing to do with the foreigners' food (thus cooks and waiters were often Muslim or Goanese, Indians who had converted to Catholicism in Portuguese Goa). Only those in lower castes could handle the family's dogs, and anything pertaining to dead animals—including the master's shoes if they were made of leather—was the province of the untouchables.

There were cooks, *kitmutgars* to serve at the table, doorkeepers, watchmen, footmen, messengers, sweepers, water carriers, gardeners, grooms and grass cutters for horses, ayahs (nannies) for the children, and many other servants. Tailors would come to the house for fittings and deliveries, and *dhobis,* who did the laundry, might live in or be hired to pick up dirty linen and bring it back fresh. Hickey eventually had a staff of 63. Like everyone else, he complained about theft and *dastur* (commissions). And like everyone else, he thoroughly enjoyed being waited on hand and foot in the grand Moghul style. After all, the number of servants one had was an indication of rank and community standing.

In mid-August, after staying for six weeks with a friend, William Hickey found a house near the courthouse. Proud of being a man of taste, he spent enormous amounts decorating it and the other houses he would live in during his Indian years. This was not an easy project, because climate limited decorating choices. "Paper or wainscot are improper, both on account of the heat, the vermin, and the difficulty of getting it done," one woman wrote. "The rooms are therefore all whited walls, but plastered in panels, which gives a pretty effect." Mirrors were a favorite wall decoration.

The heat and humidity were a constant challenge, but Hickey made his home as comfortable as he could. As was the custom, he probably cooled his house by shutting it up during the day and used a punkah, an ancient Arab device just coming into vogue. Soon to become a symbol of British India, the punkah was a large, rectangular-framed fan suspended over the dining table and moved by a cord and pulley system; power was supplied by a servant.

William also had to outfit himself and Charlotte in sufficiently fine style for going about and entertaining in society. His purchase of a London-built carriage for her, a lighter-weight phaeton for himself, and the horses to pull them—plus "wines and other liquors, always the most serious article in India"—put him in debt for 20 years.

Charlotte Hickey was now ready for the ceremony known as setting up. This was a trial imposed on all newly arrived women. Poor Charlotte, in her sympathetic partner's words, was "stuck up, full dressed, in a chair at the head of the best room . . . to receive the ladies of the settlement." There were nearly 100 lady callers, each escorted by at least two gentlemen. Another man led the group up to Charlotte and the ladies curtsied; the visitors sat for a stiff five or 10 minutes, repeated the curtsies, and left. This went on from 7 p.m. to 11 p.m., three evenings in a row. Then Charlotte had to pay return calls.

But it was by such ceremonies that the British organized their days and seasons in this foreign land. The Anglo-Indians, as they came to be called, were beginning to re-create British society amid the cycle of Indian life. Initially, the cycle was alien to the British. Hindus marked the spring in February or March with the fertility festival of Holi, which included processions and dancing. There followed a brief period when the air remained as cool as an English summer, and every tree burst into flower. Then the air heated to the furnacelike temperatures of May and June, and barbets and brain-fever birds called monotonously from their perches in the dusty trees. In June a kind of anxious anticipation began as everyone wearied of the everlasting heat and dust, the parched earth, and the wilting vegetation. People searched the clouds for signs of the coming monsoon. When the first rains broke, the earth steamed, the air rang with the songs of birds and buzzing of insects, and ecstatic people danced in the street until they were soaked.

The joy and relief were short lived as the rains continued unabated, bringing three months of torrential downpours. On days when the rain halted briefly, the respite was made miserable by clouds of mosquitoes, moths, and green flies. At last, when the rains came to an end in October, Hindus in Bengal celebrated the Durga Puja, which was held in honor of the Mother Goddess. It was dedicated to Kali (also known as Durga), who embodied the goddess in her destructive aspect, and whose temple stood at Kalighat, just south of Calcutta. The British shrank from Kali's black image with its protruding tongue and necklace of skulls, but they welcomed the misty mornings and cool, sunny days that usually followed her festival.

The concessions Europeans made to India's demanding climate were growing fewer. Some 50 years before William Hickey's time, British factors had worn comfortable, loose banian coats and flowing Moorish trousers at home and sometimes in public. But the new Anglo-Indians were bringing formality with them from home, suitable for the weather or not.

Still, in the hot season, men could dispense with their coats and wear upper and under waistcoats—one with long sleeves—in white linen for an evening visit. But the women generally kept to the full and fashionable complement of stays, shifts, stockings, petticoats, and gowns, even in 100-degree temperatures. Clothing had to be changed often, and the dhobis were kept busy washing. Hickey, however, was happy to play the part of the English gentleman and give "into the fashion with much goodwill, no person appearing in richer suits of velvet and lace than myself."

It was only in the daily schedule that Anglo-Indian Calcutta took the climate into account. People rose in the cool before dawn and often exercised before bathing. Breakfast was between 7 and 9 a.m. and in Hickey's time was changing from a simple affair of tea and toast to huge meals that included fish, meat, fowl, curries, and wine. Then men like Hickey went to their offices to work until dinnertime. Women attended to the household, read, wrote letters, or shopped in the China bazaar or "Europe shops" in the town. Sometimes, merchants would bring their wares to their customers' homes.

The dinner hour began at 2 p.m., but over time it slipped into the evening hours. The menu could be formidable, as one woman described it: "a soup, a roast fowl, curry and rice, a mutton pie, a forequarter of lamb, a rice pudding, tarts, very good cheese." As for drink, a bottle of wine per person was not unusual. After dinner the men, and occasionally the women, indulged in the hookah. William Hickey hated it, though, and assured there were men of fashion who did not smoke, he gave it up.

During the afternoon the British disappeared from the hot streets, undressed, and rested until 7 or 8 p.m., when they rose, bathed, and dressed again for airings on the course, a triangular road laid out south of the esplanade. Some rode. Some drove coaches or, like Hickey, phaetons. But coaches in Bengal were primarily for show,

In a 1786 watercolor, Calcutta's Tank Square bustles with Indians on foot and Europeans traveling about in carriages and palanquins. The Old Court House with its classical arches and the adjacent Writer's Building border the square. The Holwell obelisk, a monument to the British who perished in the Black Hole, can be seen at far left.

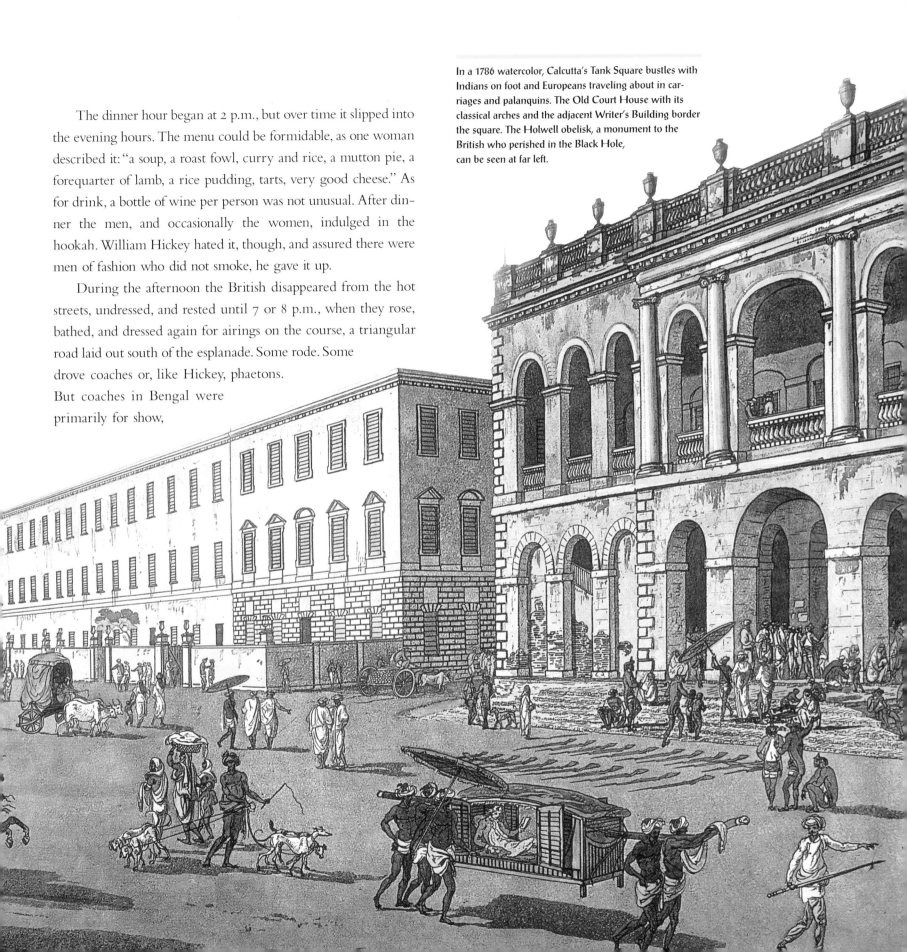

there being few decent roads. Most people traveled about in palanquins, carried by four to six liveried bearers. The litters were preceded in the daytime by servants brandishing ceremonial silver batons or, at night, by torchbearers.

After airing there was tea, and after tea, visits, perhaps with games of cards and gambling. Supper was at 10 p.m., but the convivial delights by no means ended then. For men there were taverns in the Lal Bazaar, near the north side of Tank Square, or coffeehouses, where one could read old London newspapers. Both men and women attended concerts at the Harmonic Tavern, at the edge of the bazaar. The tavern had a room for dances, which were known as assemblies. There were also subscription dances at the Calcutta The-

about—many problems were due, as one observer of British India put it, to the "gross manner in which the English live here and their excessive use of mixed liquors." Many of the sick had liver complaints. Hickey himself had chronic stomach spasms.

Although William Hickey's constitution seemed to be able to take any amount of abuse (he would live to be 80), Charlotte's health began to decline within a few months of arriving in Calcutta. At first she dismissed her anxious lover's concerns, predicting she would feel better when the cool weather came. Her physician agreed; he dismissed the violent pains in her breast as "nervous" attacks. But as William wrote years afterward, "The seeds of a fatal disease were nevertheless then lurking about her." His beloved Char-

"The seeds of a fatal disease were nevertheless then lurking about her."

atre, where ladies joined the minuet in strict order of precedence according to their husbands' ranks in the king's or company's service. And governors gave official balls and concerts with fireworks to celebrate dates such as the king's birthday, a reminder that Calcutta was a British territory.

Though the frenetic round of festive events may have been fun, it took its toll on the foreigners' health: They still suffered from all the diseases common in 18th-century England—typhoid, cholera, tuberculosis, smallpox, and scurvy, for instance—and now from tropical ailments as well. These included dysentery, parasites (such as worms), mysterious fevers, and "intermittent fevers" (malaria from living in mosquito-infested areas). Mortality from disease was high.

People blamed their illnesses on the bad air from the marshes around Calcutta. But as everyone knew—and few did anything

lotte died on Christmas Day, 1783, having survived only six months in Calcutta.

Hickey dealt with his grief the only way he knew: He drank heavily and lived hard. The worst hours were from the time he awoke, both grieving and hung over, until he got to business at his desk. Although he managed to have the occasional good time getting drunk, in the end, parties were not enough.

William Hickey yearned for the type of companionship he had enjoyed with Charlotte and finally found it with an intelligent, charming, and attractive Indian woman named Jemdanee. Following a precedent set by many nabobs before him, he brought the young woman into his home to share his life. She lived with him for years, happily it seems, for he described her as "respected and admired by all my friends by her extraordinary sprightliness and good humour." He built her a garden house about 25 miles

upriver in the Dutch settlement of Chinsura, to which he traveled on his own boat.

So the years passed for Hickey. He continued his rollicking ways with his drinking friends, served in various official capacities, and continued to observe life around him with interest, taking note of quarrels, murders, executions, changes of government style, and the imprisonment of Indian princes by the British. When Jemdanee died in child-birth in 1796, he grieved deeply. The wife of Hickey's business partner suggested that Hickey and Jemdanee's son be given into her care, and "she received him as if her own." Despite his surrogate mother's loving attentions, the infant died nine months later, mourned by his father as "the only living memento of my lamented favorite."

Clothed in the finest European fashions, British shoppers stroll through Calcutta's Taylor's Emporium in search of china, chandeliers, urns, and paintings; the Indian porters are the only sign that this is not England. Shopping at Taylor's was a favorite pastime for well-to-do Anglo-Indians in the 1820s.

THE

CALCUTTA GAZETTE;

OR,

ORIENTAL ADVERTISER.

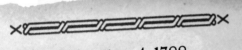

December 4, 1788

Mr. Gairard does himself the pleasure to acquaint the Ladies and Gentlemen of Calcutta, that his Vauxhall Exhibition of Fire-works will commence this day, Thursday, the 4th instant, by a grand display Entitled 'The Garden of Pleasure.' The Garden is laid out in very great order, with the additional advantage of new walks, all covered in, to protect the company from the vapours of the evening, and when illuminated, will afford a very pleasing *Coup D'Oeil*. The Fire-works will commence at eight o'clock precisely.

April 19, 1792

Three royal tigers were killed last week at Sooksagur by Mr. Baretto, one of which having seized a man very near his elephant, he shot him dead on the spot; the other two were taken in nets.

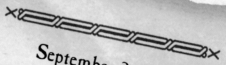

September 3, 1789

An influenza has for some time past been general among the European inhabitants of Calcutta. A medical correspondent recommends to those who can afford it to "drink deep" in rosy-port, not so as "to forget all their care," but so as to guard them against the bad effects of that unwholesome weather which ever attends the breaking up of the rains, by a good and comfortable living.

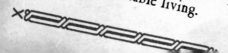

The News of the Day

Launched in March 1784, the *Calcutta Gazette* sought to publish political and social news of the day for the British. Calcutta's first newspaper, the *Bengal Gazette,* inaugurated just four years earlier, had folded due to vitriolic attacks on British officials by its editor, James Hicky. Officials shut down the paper and threw Hicky in prison for libel. Decidedly less controversial, the *Calcutta Gazette* enjoyed a long run, publishing twice weekly until 1832.

The newspaper was divided into several subsections. The official portion printed articles on public policy, extracts from Acts of Parliament, or minutes from local council meetings, one approving a contract to a Mr. W. Fairlie to supply and feed 200 elephants and 90 camels required for the British army in 1799. The editorial section varied from hard news to such items as the announcement of a daylong celebration of the king's birthday in 1792. The Poet's Corner featured patriotic odes, ballads, or witticisms, and the advertisements section ran the gamut from public auctions and sales of European goods to real estate and employment opportunities; a sampling of such ads is pictured on these pages. Reading the *Gazette,* it is clear that Calcutta experienced its share of traumas and entertainments—from murders, robberies, duels, abductions, and elopements to cricket matches, pony races, balls, and theatrical performances.

October 30, 1788

Lafleur, Hair-Dresser to Ladies and Gentlemen, being lately come from Paris, dresses hair according to the latest fashion. He takes four Rupees for dressing a Lady. Two Rupees for a Gentleman. And six Rupees for cutting hair. In case any Ladies or Gentlemen would wish to hire him per month, he will settle with them at a very reasonable rate.

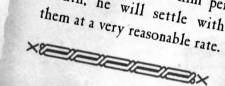

February 16, 1786

Whereas, I, John Ghent, being on the Race Ground on Monday, the 30th of January 1786, did, without provocation, strike Mr. Robert Hays, I, in this public manner, beg pardon of the said Mr. Hays for committing the aforesaid offence.

March 21, 1799

To parents and guardians. Mrs. Middleton begs leave to inform her friends and the public, that having taken a house in an airy, healthy, and agreeable situation at Dinapore, she proposes keeping a school for the tuition of such young gentlemen and ladies as parents or guardians may think proper to commit to her charge; who may be assured that the strictest attention shall be paid to their health, morals, and every branch of education.

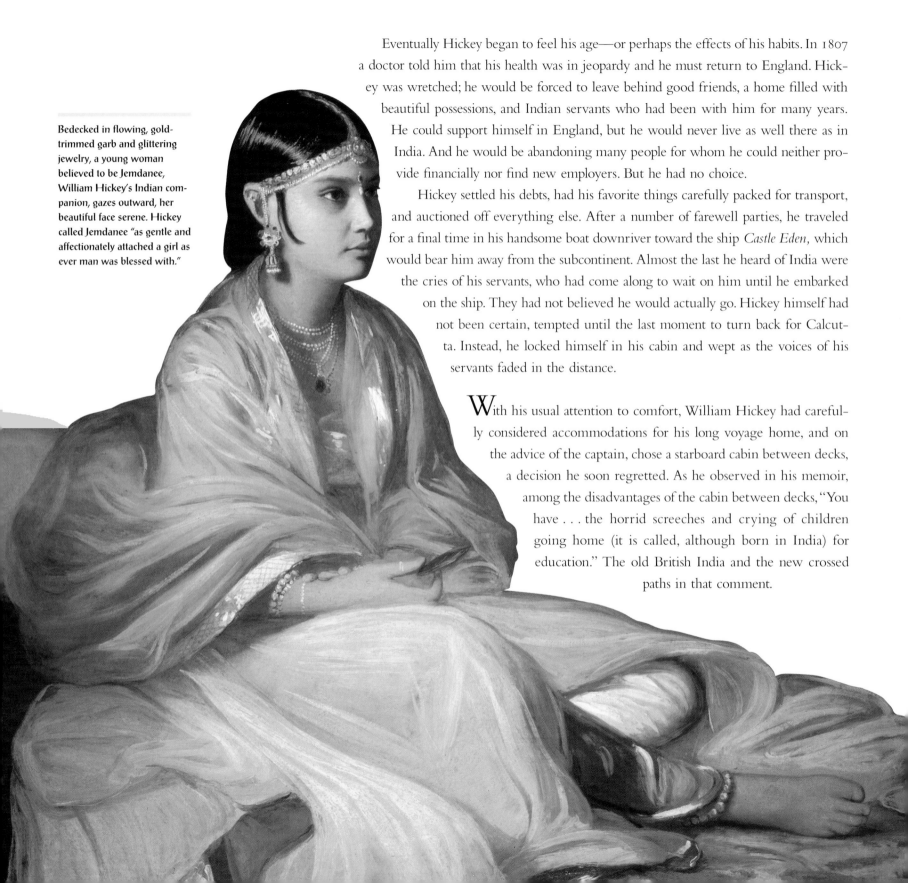

Bedecked in flowing, gold-trimmed garb and glittering jewelry, a young woman believed to be Jemdanee, William Hickey's Indian companion, gazes outward, her beautiful face serene. Hickey called Jemdanee "as gentle and affectionately attached a girl as ever man was blessed with."

Eventually Hickey began to feel his age—or perhaps the effects of his habits. In 1807 a doctor told him that his health was in jeopardy and he must return to England. Hickey was wretched; he would be forced to leave behind good friends, a home filled with beautiful possessions, and Indian servants who had been with him for many years. He could support himself in England, but he would never live as well there as in India. And he would be abandoning many people for whom he could neither provide financially nor find new employers. But he had no choice.

Hickey settled his debts, had his favorite things carefully packed for transport, and auctioned off everything else. After a number of farewell parties, he traveled for a final time in his handsome boat downriver toward the ship *Castle Eden*, which would bear him away from the subcontinent. Almost the last he heard of India were the cries of his servants, who had come along to wait on him until he embarked on the ship. They had not believed he would actually go. Hickey himself had not been certain, tempted until the last moment to turn back for Calcutta. Instead, he locked himself in his cabin and wept as the voices of his servants faded in the distance.

With his usual attention to comfort, William Hickey had carefully considered accommodations for his long voyage home, and on the advice of the captain, chose a starboard cabin between decks, a decision he soon regretted. As he observed in his memoir, among the disadvantages of the cabin between decks, "You have . . . the horrid screeches and crying of children going home (it is called, although born in India) for education." The old British India and the new crossed paths in that comment.

With the turn of the century, people such as William Hickey began to be out of place. In the new British Raj, as British-ruled India was known, the settlements consisted of fewer young men on their own trying to strike it rich or make a name for themselves, and greater numbers of bureaucrats and their families. There were schools in Calcutta where children of full British or mixed parentage could receive an education, but as Hickey found, any family who could possibly afford it sent their children home for a proper British education at age seven. The British writer of an Indian guidebook expressed the opinion of many when he stated that although the teaching in the schools in India was sufficient, he would never send a child there. "All so educated, are rendered unfit for the society of gentlemen who have been brought up in Europe." An education in India could ruin a young woman's marriage prospects and a young man's career opportunities. Yet only a minority of parents had the money to send their children abroad, and a large number of British children born in India in those early years did not even live to the age of seven.

Anglo-Indian families coped as well as they could. Such a family was that of Mary Martha Sherwood and her husband, Captain Henry Sherwood, paymaster to a royal infantry regiment, who was sent to India with his troops in 1805. Mary Martha, then 30, left her adored 11-month-old daughter in her own mother's care in order to be with him. Tall, auburn haired, and pretty, Mary Martha Sherwood had been brought up in the enlightened atmosphere of an Anglican country rectory—her father was chaplain to George III for a while—by cultured parents, who gave her a golden childhood. Although she may have had to do her lessons strapped to a backboard to prevent slouching, as was customary for girls of the time, she was educated along with her brother in Latin and Greek, given the run of her father's library, and set free to enjoy the Worcestershire countryside when classes were over. A happy young life and a close and happy marriage to her cousin Henry kept Sherwood's spirit warm and loving.

After her father died, she was drawn to the religious evangelical movement, then coming into its own in England. This fervent and growing group insisted on the intrinsic evil of the human heart, the importance of good works, and the rejection of a range of temptations—from idolatry to worldly pleasures.

Although Sherwood later softened her views, evangelical beliefs colored her every experience and all her writing.

In India she moved with her husband as his regiment was transferred to encampments scattered across the north. Life on the military posts was very different from that of Calcutta—more insular, with fewer resources. The posts were designed around squares, bordered by soldiers' barracks and officers' quarters. Officers' quarters were in the style of India: single-story buildings with shady, overhanging roofs adapted from Indian dwellings and known as bungalows (a corruption of the word *bangla,* meaning Bengali). Their bare, whitewashed rooms were high and echoing, built for coolness, with tall, green-shuttered windows and verandas overlooking the squares, the countryside, or private gardens. Servants' houses—the Sherwoods had the usual complement of servants—lay behind the bungalows. Not far from each post was the bustle of a native town and bazaar.

Once settled at each post, Sherwood threw herself into work. She started schools on her verandas for the soldiers' children; she studied the Bible; she wrote steadily, not only a journal but the moral stories that would make her reputation as an author back in England. Wearing the light white dresses and lace caps then in style, she joined in each post's little social round of church and dinner parties. On Christmas Day, 1805, she gave birth to a son, Henry, at Dinapore.

The next year, still weak from childbirth, she moved with the regiment to Berhampore. River and jungle surrounded the encampment: "The whole country steamed like a brewing vat," she said, and the result was that the British on the post were languid, weak, and pale. Nevertheless, she continued her writing and set up a new school.

As was the custom, Sherwood had Indian wet nurses and ayahs for her children. Sherwood fired one ayah for giving Henry opium to keep him quiet and had hysterical scenes with another who took him to a Hindu ceremony where he was given a

painted mark on his forehead: a "spot set on his brow by a minister of Satan." Others, though, tended her children not only to her satisfaction but with a kindness she would never forget.

After Henry was weaned, he grew thin, pale, and fretful. Henry's ayah, a former singer and dancer, held the boy and sang him lullabies for hours on end as she walked up and down the family's veranda. "Her voice was sweet, and a more affectionate creature I never knew," Sherwood recalled, and in the years to follow, the Englishwoman would sing the ayah's songs "to every little one who rested on my knee." Then, all the children on the post, including Henry, contracted whooping cough. Henry lasted for weeks, but it became clear that he was failing.

During this time, Sherwood bore another child, Lucy Martha. But the happiness of the birth would be followed by greater sorrow. One Saturday Sherwood carried her son toward the river, pointing out the elephants on the banks to amuse him. Later that day, as he lay near death, his family kept vigil. At one point, Sherwood wrote, "he turned his lovely eyes to me and smiled." Then he was gone. His mother grieved deeply, but drew comfort from Lucy, all dimples and sleepy blue eyes. The next year at Cawnpore, the little girl also died, after months of suffering from dysentery. Sherwood was devastated, and in her despair became convinced that she had been punished for loving Lucy too much: "My God was preparing me to give up this idol also."

The deaths of her children seemed to draw Mary Martha Sherwood deeper into the evangelical fold, and she absorbed its prejudices. Many evangelicals regarded Indian culture as corrupt and degraded and its people as idolators—ideas that would permeate Anglo-Indian attitudes as the century wore on. On the one hand, Sherwood could delight in the beauty of the landscape and describe the local inhabitants as "delicately formed . . . mild, calm, and naturally polite." But she was also capable of the most abusive language when discussing the culture and people around her. Though she learned Hindustani to deal with household servants and promote the teachings of the Bible, she learned nothing of India's scholarship and philosophy. Like other women in her position, she had little opportunity to meet educated or high-caste Hindus. And she was revolted by the subcontinent's arts, especially in the holy city of Benares. "Horrible and disproportioned figures," she wrote, "similitudes of the gods of their depraved imaginations, painted on the walls of buildings or carved in stone or wood, occur in every direction."

Yet Sherwood took the doctrine of salvation by good works seriously and, where prejudice did not blind her, had a kind heart. There was the matter of soldiers' families, for instance. Whether the mothers were British or Indian, they and their children generally lived wretched lives. Their quarters in India were no more than screened-off cor-

A British boy runs to his nanny, or ayah, while a wet nurse suckles a baby; in the background is a bed covered by mosquito netting. In wealthy households, each child might have his or her own ayah and would be watched over by other servants as well. Famed children's author Mary Martha Sherwood *(right)* employed ayahs for her offspring, but some British were afraid that their children would be spoiled by Indian caretakers, who were reportedly gentler and less stern than British nannies.

ners of the barracks, producing squalid conditions in which their children—"barracks rats"—seldom thrived and were often abused. There were no schools for them, except those run by Sherwood. At her schools, which began with religious instruction, everyone was welcome. "I refused none who came to ask me to receive and instruct their little ones, not even when the children were colored." Barracks rats, officers' children, and the offspring of local Indians all attended her schools.

Sherwood adopted sad cases from the barracks, partly out of kindness and partly to comfort herself for her own lost children. One was a little girl named Annie, whose mother had died. Annie's caretaker, Sherwood discovered, had been dosing her with gin. Sherwood immediately took the girl into her own home. Another, in Cawnpore, was Sally, who had also lost her mother and come under the care of an abusive guardian. Sherwood ordered Sally brought for an examination and found the two-year-

old had clearly been starved. Outraged, Sherwood took over Sally's care. Luckily, the little girl improved steadily. Sherwood organized a fund to care for other barracks orphans and helped to make clothes for them.

The Sherwoods' routine at Cawnpore was busy and creative. Their quarters were large and shady, with beautiful gardens. In the early summer season of fierce, hot winds, every outer door and window was shuttered, and tatties—woven screens of sweet-smelling vetiver grass, kept wet by servants—were wrapped around the windward side, to cool the air. Husband and wife worked in the cavernous hall of the house in the mornings, in "what lovers of broad daylight would call almost darkness, whilst we heard no sounds but the monotonous click of the punkah, or the melancholy moaning of the burning blast without." At one o'clock there would be a hot dinner of curry and vegetables. After that everyone rested. At four they drank

The image of Jagannatha, a form of the god Vishnu, stands within a replica of his temple mounted on a huge cart. Hindu celebrants, joined by an Indian nobleman and a British couple atop elephants, parade through the streets of the city of Puri during the annual Rath Yatra, or Cart Procession. Worshipers sometimes showed their devotion by throwing themselves under the cart's wheels.

coffee, bathed, and dressed. At six, when the winds usually fell, the servants took the tatties down and opened the house, and in the evenings, the Sherwood family went for drives or sat on the veranda. There was neither dancing nor card playing and very little entertainment.

There was, however, reading and writing. Mary Martha Sherwood kept diaries. More than that, she wrote religious tracts and fiction that suited the mood of the times. Because her moral tales of bad children and good, and of punishments and rewards, were lively, with sharply observed scenes and vivid characters, they became bestsellers. Hers was a hardworking life, vastly different from that of most British women in India. In true evangelical mode, she learned and taught, improved herself, and certainly improved the lot of others.

In August 1809 Mary Martha Sherwood bore another daughter, Lucy Elizabeth. The regimental physician had told her after her other daughter's death that she must take any future children to England if she expected them to survive. Henry and Mary Martha prepared for separation reluctantly, for they were a close and loving couple. In October they took the month-long trip down the Ganges and Hooghly Rivers from Cawnpore to Calcutta, placing Annie and Sally en route with people they trusted, so mother and daughter could board a ship for home.

But in Calcutta, the couple found they could not face life apart. They spoke in the night: "He was in a state of the deepest grief, and then he told me that he absolutely could not bear the thought of my leaving him." So Mary Martha proposed that they take young Lucy to the best physicians in Calcutta to see whether more eminent men agreed with the regimental doctor. They did not, opining it would be safe for Lucy to stay in India for a few years.

The delighted couple journeyed home, once again traveling by water. India's vast riverine network was the fastest, safest, most comfortable way to move about. Whole regiments like Captain Sherwood's changed posts that way, traveling with all the people, armaments, animals, and provisions that follow an army. This time, the Sherwoods traveled with no companions besides tiny Lucy, their servants, and the boatmen, and the journey turned into a kind of honeymoon as they settled into the slow rhythms of a 16-week meander toward Cawnpore.

River travel was one of the arts of British India. Houseboats known as budgerows and pinnaces made it a pleasure. Moved by sails or by oarsmen, called dandies, such houseboats had the same general layout. There were three rooms in the stern: a veranda toward the bow, a hall or living room that might measure 16 feet long by 14 feet wide, then a bedroom. A deck in front of the rooms provided space for the dandies. The helmsman at the stern guided the rudder; another person stood at the prow and used a long oar to ascertain river depth. The bow was ornamented with a carved bird or fish.

The Sherwoods' pinnace was reserved for them and close servants like Lucy's ayah. Baggage boats and a cooking boat with supplies like wine, flour, salted butter in casks, and chickens and goats followed. A little wherry for getting from one boat to another bobbed along behind. All day long the Sherwoods would sail the river, writing, reading, or simply observing the passing scene of India. They wandered first through the Ganges delta jungle known as the Sundarbans, thronged with ospreys, ibises, storks, and kingfishers, as well as with crocodiles and water snakes. Sometimes monkeys peered from the foliage. At night the couple heard the wailing of jackals and, once, the howl of a tiger—from their safe anchor in the middle of the stream.

At sunset, the boats would anchor, and all the servants, except those attending to the Sherwoods' dinner on the cook's boat, would go ashore. The Indians, separating into groups, would build fires for dinner. "Each mess, according to its caste or family, has one cook appointed. These cooks bring out their bags of rice and all things needful, and begin without delay to concoct." Meanwhile, "the dhoby brings his simple apparatus from his boat and begins to wash his master's linen in the river; another servant brings out the goats to browse on the bank; the head man goes off to forage in the nearest bazaar."

The Sherwoods would have gone for a short walk before returning for their own meal, replete with tablecloth, crystal, and china. It was a river idyll Mary Martha Sherwood would long remember—not only the time spent with her husband, but that spent with Lucy as well. "In her," the grateful mother wrote, "I seemed to have found again all the children I had lost."

By February they had reached Mirzapur, where they stayed with judge and magistrate George Ricketts. The Rickettses had three or four children at school in England and four at home, who lived in their own wing of the huge house: "Each child in this establishment had two or more servants," Mary Martha Sherwood noted, "and over all these was a large, tall, consequential, superbly dressed, high-salaried white woman, a sergeant's widow, who sat in state, gave her orders."

The Rickettses' six-year-old daughter Louisa was still at home, always attended by servants who indulged her every whim. She was completely undisciplined, Sherwood remarked sternly: "She had never been taught even her letters, she had never been set down to any task." When the adults tried to have a conversation, Louisa burst in on them and treated them to a headstand. Her parents called out, *Koi hai?* (Is someone there?)—the usual way of summoning servants, who bore her kicking and laughing away.

Sherwood also noted that the Rickettses' children looked

plump and well—not like most Anglo-Indian children. Not content with advice from the sergeant's widow, the anxious mother consulted the children's old ayah about Lucy's health. The ayah's advice was to keep the child with a wet nurse until she had cut every tooth, a daunting prospect for the wet nurse, perhaps, but advice Sherwood followed for the rest of her stay.

Not long before they had arrived at the Rickettses' home, the Sherwoods passed another British family on the Ganges. As was the custom, all stopped for greetings. In the other boat was the family that had taken Sally. To prevent the little girl from getting above her lowly birth, the new guardians and their servants treated her coldly. They had even dressed her poorly, replacing her pretty muslin frock with a kind of chintz wrap-

In the northeastern town of Chapra, a European-style mansion overlooks a landscaped lawn and garden with towering trellises, tended by *malis,* or Indian gardeners *(foreground and center).* Well-to-do Anglo-Indians in the provinces often modeled their homes after the "marble palaces" owned by wealthy British in Calcutta.

89

per with long, loose sleeves. Captain Sherwood found Sally in this costume, "her little face all anxiety and baby care." To Sally's great happiness, he returned her to his wife. They would have taken Annie back, as well, but she was prospering in her new household, clearly beloved.

Mary Martha Sherwood would never be content with only two children. By 1816, when the Sherwoods decided it was time to return to their homeland, they had seven—counting their eldest daughter, left in England 10 years before; Lucy; three children safely born in the Sherwoods' final years in India; and two adopted orphans. She left behind other soldiers' children she had found homes for and, thanks to much hard work, an official orphanage. It was in many ways a sad leave-taking for the Sherwood family. "These poor babies were about to leave their native country," Mary Martha said of her children. "They then spoke little English; all their conversation passed in Hindustani, all their associations were Oriental." It was not only difficult for the children. "I had a dread of leaving India," confided Sherwood. "I had long loved the country."

Sherwood would spend the rest of her life caring for children—with her husband, she ran a boarding school for many years—and writing for them. As she aged, her religious and cultural views softened. She no longer believed that Indians should "live according to such views of right and wrong as I had myself." Even in India, she had sometimes set aside her cultural prejudices and shared emotions with the Indians who surrounded her. She recalled a tender meeting with her dead son's ayah, who wept for him with her. "There are moments of intense feeling," she once

As artisans spin and weave *(foreground)*, mythological scientist Idris *(seated)*, credited with introducing weaving to the world, accepts finished rolls of cloth. Indian artisans in the third millennium BC may have been the first to perfect the art of weaving.

Clothed in a cotton gown embroidered with colored silk and silver thread, Captain John Foote of the East India Company celebrates his connection to India in a 1765 portrait.

Web of the Woven Wind

Though the English had initially been drawn to India by the spice trade, textiles soon became the major export. Using handlooms and spindles and building on a 5,000-year history of weaving, Indian artisans created such fine fabrics that one 19th-century Briton characterized them as "the work of fairies or insects rather than of men."

From yarn described as the "web of the woven wind," Bengali weavers produced delicate cotton muslins so sheer that they were named "running water" and "evening dew." Silk brocades from the city of Benares in northern India glittered with threads of gold or silver. In Kashmir, enormous shawls—so finely woven that they could be drawn through a ring—were made from the inner fleece of a rare mountain goat, which left its hairs behind when it rubbed against shrubs on Himalayan peaks. Indian chintz—calico that was hand painted or printed by artisans—was renowned for brilliant colors that seemed to improve with repeated washings.

A rage for Indian fabric swept across Britain, causing a serious drain of gold and silver from the West. "From the greatest gallants to the meanest Cook Maids, nothing was thought so fit to adorn their persons as

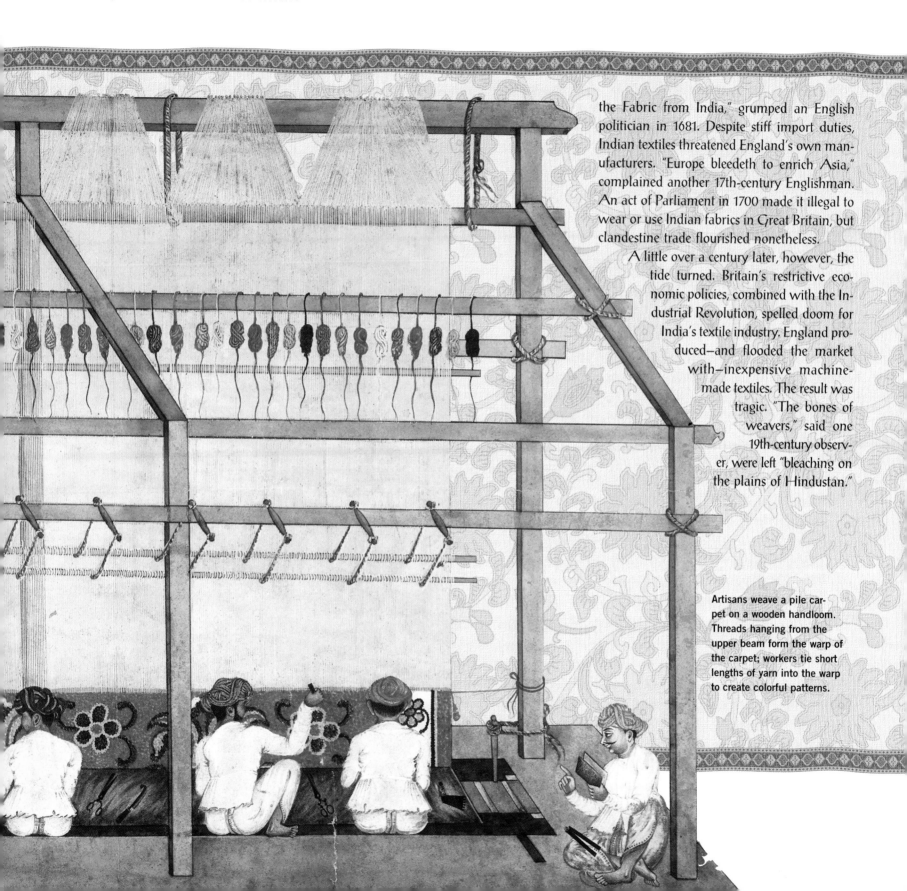

the Fabric from India," grumped an English politician in 1681. Despite stiff import duties, Indian textiles threatened England's own manufacturers. "Europe bleedeth to enrich Asia," complained another 17th-century Englishman. An act of Parliament in 1700 made it illegal to wear or use Indian fabrics in Great Britain, but clandestine trade flourished nonetheless.

A little over a century later, however, the tide turned. Britain's restrictive economic policies, combined with the Industrial Revolution, spelled doom for India's textile industry. England produced—and flooded the market with—inexpensive machine-made textiles. The result was tragic. "The bones of weavers," said one 19th-century observer, were left "bleaching on the plains of Hindustan."

Artisans weave a pile carpet on a wooden handloom. Threads hanging from the upper beam form the warp of the carpet; workers tie short lengths of yarn into the warp to create colorful patterns.

The 18th-century European dress at right was fashioned out of painted and dyed chintz from southeast India's Coromandel Coast. The design was painted by hand with a soft steel-wire brush. Less-expensive chintz was made by printers like the one above, who is pressing a wooden block dipped in dye onto a length of fabric.

wrote, "in which all distinctions of nations, colours, and castes disappear, and in their place there only remains between two human beings one abiding sense of common nature."

As the 19th century progressed, British power and population increased; the Moghul empire shrank to an impotent enclave around Delhi; and independent princes, one by one, became British clients. British attitudes toward Indians continued to change. Governors general from Charles Cornwallis onward closed the door to mutual cooperation. Indian participation in government was reduced to an absolute minimum; social interactions, even with Muslim royalty, were limited and distant. The British began to see—and treat—all Indians as an inferior and conquered people, and to make maintenance of British power and aloofness a policy. The spread of the evangelical movement, with its horror of the non-Christian, only added to Britons' concepts of their inherent superiority.

The change was gradual, but it was noticeable, particularly among the many women—the memsahibs, as the mistresses of European households were respectfully called—arriving in India. As recently as the early 1800s, there had been women who spoke Hindustani and had friends among their Indian counterparts, secluded in the zenana, or women's quarters. But a Mrs. Graham, newly arrived in Calcutta in 1810, observed that she was unable to make friends with native families, as she had before in Bombay. "This mixture of nations ought, I think, to weaken national prejudices, but among the English, at least, the effect seems to be diametrically opposite," she wrote. By 1830 memsahibs had few Indian contacts, except for servants, and it was considered bad taste to wear anything of Indian manufacture. One Englishwoman in Madras was asked what she had seen of India and its people. "Oh, nothing," she blithely replied. "Thank goodness, I know nothing at all about them . . . I think the less one sees and knows of them, the better."

Still, there were some British people who lacked the prejudices and conventions of the Victorian middle class that now ruled India. Some were aristocrats who could afford to ignore convention. Others were simply strong and independent—such as Fanny Parks. Fanny was the wife of Charles Parks, who was collector of customs in Allahabad—at the confluence of the Ganges and the Jumna Rivers, in north-central India—for much of the time between 1826 and 1845.

Fanny was an army officer's daughter, and Charles came from a family with a tradition of Indian service, and they had a network of friends all over the subcontinent. This was fortunate, because Fanny Parks was a tireless traveler and a superb horsewoman who liked adventure. She was interested in science, in music, in handicrafts, and in languages. Most of all she liked the romance of India, of its fabled scenery and dramatic weather, its fallen greatness, and its colorful present.

Even the difficulties of life in the tropics left Fanny Parks undaunted. Like everyone else, she complained during the hot season, but she also used the latest inventions (and her 57 servants) to combat it. She had punkahs and tatties, painted her walls French gray for coolness, and must have been among the first to install a human-powered air coolant device called the thermantidote. A structure "awful to behold," as she told her mother, the thermantidote was an enormous cylinder whose sides were fitted with dampened tatties and whose interior held large, revolving fans. It stood against an exterior house wall, with a funnel projecting into

THE LURE OF OPIUM

"As opium is prohibited by the Chinese Government," wrote East India Company directors in the 1760s, "introducing it there can only be in a clandestine manner." Such qualms about breaking Chinese law soon disappeared. Selling opium to China was highly profitable, helping to pay for the vast amounts of tea England imported from there.

After sowing the poppy seeds in company-owned fields each November, Indian workers harvested the raw opium in March by cutting an incision in the seed head. Growers then transported the gummy sap to processing plants, where it was made into two-pound balls or cakes and wrapped in poppy leaves. At left, workers stack opium onto racks for drying in a huge warehouse holding some 300,000 balls. They turned the balls periodically, dusting and examining them for bugs and mildew before packing them into crates and sending them to China. Alarmed by the growing number of opium addicts, the Chinese government passed edicts to ban opium import, but corrupt Chinese officials looked the other way.

a room. Servants kept the tatties wet and turned the handles that moved the fans, forcing cooled air into the house.

There was little defense, however, against the irritating insects, snakes, and animals of the tropics. For protection from mosquitoes, beds were draped with netting and ladies sometimes wore canvas boots under their dinner dresses to protect their legs. Setting the legs of furniture in little tubs of water helped protect against the ubiquitous white ants, which devoured furniture, books, and clothing. But there was little one could do when they swarmed. "These ants, at a certain period after a shower, rise from the earth with four large wings," Parks wrote, and they would swarm about the lamps, putting them out in minutes.

There were hordes of moths at night, dung beetles the size of walnuts, and most sickening of all, stink bugs. Writing in her journal, Parks noted, "They are odious; they fly upon your face and arms, and into your plate; if you brush them away, they emit such terrible effluvia it is sickening, and yet one cannot bear them to crawl over one's body, as one is this minute doing on my ear."

In a spirit of scientific inquiry, Fanny Parks collected these exotica, until the bungalow in Allahabad became a kind of natural history museum. Charles took it in stride: "She is deeply read in taxidermy, and we have, besides, many other prepared subjects, such as tigers, and hyenas' skulls, alligator's skeleton whole, a delightful little pet in spirits of wine, a young crocodile, skin and all." There was, in addition, "the 'Bottle of Horrors!' containing cobra de capello, scorpions, lizards, millepieds, centpieds, grillus monstrosus, and I know not what." Charles went on calmly smoking his cigar, "as happy as if I was one of the party in the bottle, the daily object of admiration!"

Everything about India interested the Englishwoman. Parks learned Hindustani and Persian, and she studied the sitar. She tried opium for pain and found that it not only cured the pain but made her happy (and even more talkative than usual). She chewed pan and found it "very refreshing." And she loved Indian food.

Like most Europeans, she was fascinated by such extreme Hindu practices as sati, widows burning to death on their husbands' funeral pyres, and thuggee, ritual murder in honor of the goddess Kali. She never saw an act of sati, because it was rare, but she sketched some commemorative mounds on a riverbank where it had occurred. "The family who owned the large mound kept it in repair," Parks noted, "and were very proud of the glory reflected on their house by one of the females having become sati."

Parks seems to have written down everything she could find out about thuggee, the practice then being suppressed by Captain William Sleeman of the Bengal Army. And then there was hook

swinging—a penitential rite dedicated to Shiva, god of destruction. Devotees were attached to revolving poles by wires threaded through their chests and shoulder blades, then swung in circles in the air. Parks observed it, reporting calmly, "I was much disgusted, but greatly interested."

Most of all, Fanny Parks traveled, often alone except for servants. About 10 months after Parks settled in Allahabad, a friend invited her north to Lucknow because the British commander in chief in India, Lord Combermere, was visiting. She accepted with alacrity: Everyone wanted to see Lucknow, where the nawab of Oudh still lived in splendor, Moghul style. Lucknow's British resident, or top official, was ensconced in a 33-acre walled compound at the town's center. British residencies existed in all the capitals of the native princes who had subsidiary alliances with the British, but Lucknow's residency was distinguished by its size. The British enclave was a grand space, dominated by the residency itself, a building so tall one could see out over the lawns and gardens to

Swinging on hooks embedded in their backs and chests, five men throw sweetmeats and flowers to a crowd during a religious festival *(top)*. Fanny Parks, who drew the scene, described one man as "very wild, from the quantity of opium and bengh [or bhang, an intoxicating liquor] he had taken to deaden the sense of pain." She also sketched this elephant fight *(left)*, where a driver was crushed to death.

the domes and towers of the native city, itself the last word in luxury. True, the poorer quarters huddled up against the residency walls were the usual maze of alleys and bazaars. But the river Gumti flowed to the north, and by it stood the vast palace of the nawab. There were splendid gardens with pavilions in the airy Moghul style. The palace itself had a many-storied gate, from the top of which drum bands saluted visiting dignitaries. Inside, under glittering, gilded domes were huge, arched rooms and vaulted halls. Everywhere was the emblem of the fish, the special insignia of the dynasty.

The nawab maintained an opulent court, where some of the talent of dying Moghul India had fled. Lucknow was famous for its medicine, its art—especially its calligraphy—its music, and its dance. Most spectacularly, it was famous for its animal fights. The rulers of Oudh maintained vast menageries: Across the Gumti was a royal stable for 150 fighting elephants. But the nawab also had fighting tigers, rhinoceroses, camels (these, not normally fighters, had to be specially trained), horses, cocks, and quails. Fanny Parks was positively agog.

She stayed first at the residency, whose incumbent was an old friend, and so she was included in the official party that attended the ceremonial breakfast the nawab gave for Lord Combermere. After the meal, the residency party was taken to a room where trays of presents were spread upon the floor, chosen according to the guests' rank. Parks had two trays, "the first containing several pairs of Cashmere shawls, and a pile of India muslin, and *kimkhwab,* or cloth of gold. The other tray contained strings of pearl, precious stones, bracelets, and other beautiful native jewelry." But the East India Company now had strict rules about presents, and all gifts were later placed in the company's treasury.

What Parks really wanted to see was the animal fights. Fortunately, mornings at Lucknow were devoted to sports. She found the quail fights very entertaining: Two little quail cocks were put on a table with a hen nearby, and Parks wrote, "they set to instantly and fought valiantly. One of the quails was driven back by his adversary, until the little bird, who fought every inch of his forced retreat, fell off the table into my lap."

What she did not see was Lucknow's royal zenana—the separate women's quarters that the Moghuls introduced to India. But Parks would have plenty of opportunities to explore zenanas. Among them, her favorite—partly because she was sympathetic to Hinduism and partly because she admired strong women—was probably that of Baiza Bai.

The queen of Gwalior, Baiza Bai, had assumed the reins of state upon the death of her husband. But by 1835 she had become a virtual prisoner of the British government after seeking its protection two years before, when her subjects rebelled. As it happened, Parks had a relative serving as a judge at Fatehgarh, near where the queen lived in an elaborate camp. Parks visited Fatehgarh and soon became a welcome visitor at the queen's camp, no doubt because of her fluency in Hindustani, her care in following rules of Indian etiquette, and her willingness to satisfy the queen's curiosity about British women.

She found the queen seated on a *gaddi*—an embroidered cushion of state placed on the floor—with a throng of ladies-in-waiting. One of the women carried a sword and accompanied the queen wherever she went. In attendance also was Baiza Bai's granddaughter, the gaja raja sahib. Her title was a masculine one, unusual in India, but not in Baiza Bai's family, where the women usually held such titles. Baiza Bai was heavy and gray haired and had a sweet smile and an exceptionally attractive voice. "There is a freedom and independence in her air that I greatly admire," wrote Parks.

Being a widow, Baiza Bai was plainly dressed in red silk with no ornament other than a pair of gold bracelets—a great contrast to the pearls and diamonds worn by her granddaughter. Parks found the women's dress exceptionally graceful. It consisted of a tight blouse and a skirt made of 20 yards of silk, wrapped around the body and then part of it drawn between the legs and fastened in back, to produce "the effect both of petticoat and trousers."

Parks also discovered how convenient the costume was when the queen asked her to demonstrate riding sidesaddle. (The ladies of Gwalior were renowned horsewomen. The queen, it was said, had ridden into battle at the head of her troops, with a lance in her hand and an infant on her arm.) Parks borrowed a beautiful Arabian steed belonging to her British host and adorned him with a garland of jasmine. "I mounted him and entering the precincts of the zenana, found myself in a large court, where all the ladies of the ex-Queen were assembled, and anxiously looking for the English lady who would ride crooked!"

When the women had examined the horse with expert attention, Parks put him dashingly through his paces. Then female attendants brought in three of the queen's riding horses. Velvet and gold brocade and embroidery covered the saddles while precious jewels and gold chains draped the animals' heads and necks. "The Gaja Raja, in her riding dress, mounted one of the horses, and the ladies the others; they cantered and pranced

In a room of a zenana, or segregated women's quarters, a group of women amuse themselves on a large swing while their companions watch. Other than husbands, men were prohibited from entering these apartments. Under no such restriction, Fanny Parks eagerly visited the zenanas of well-to-do commoners, princesses, and a former queen.

about, showing off their style of riding." They challenged Parks to ride astride and, changing her black habit for a borrowed trouser skirt, she did. Riding astride was so safe that she felt she could jump over the moon.

In the days and months that followed, the women exchanged views, questions, and even jokes. How could men have made English laws, the queen inquired mischievously, and permit themselves only one wife? Parks replied in kind that England was so small that if each man had four wives and followed the Indian rules about giving them separate establishments, the island could never contain them.

A round of visits followed: Parks entertained the queen on her own pinnace, carefully setting up screens to maintain purdah, the traditional seclusion of women from public view. She taught the gaja raja how to make tea. Parks was invited to a wedding, and she found herself contrasting her own European clothes with the graceful robes of her hostess: "We flatter ourselves we are well dressed, but in our hideous European ungraceful attire we are a blot in the procession."

Goodwill, curiosity, and tact on both sides led to a friendship that lasted the rest of Parks's years in India. When Baiza Bai was transferred to Allahabad, for instance, Parks helped her give a dinner party for the British, translating for the guests, most of whom did not speak Hindustani, and helping them deal with the purdah curtain that divided the room and concealed the hostess. When the Englishwoman traveled, the queen sent her *kharitas*—letters enclosed in bags of crimson silk embroidered and tied with gold. Later, when Parks departed for leave in England, the old queen wept to see her go.

Bolstered by their English protectors, the nawab of Oudh and even the captive queen still lived in the royal style that Parks expected. But it took a trip to Delhi in 1838 for her to see the tattered reality of what had become of the great Moghul empire. Delhi had been the seat of Indian rulers from the ancient, mythic past; from the 17th century, it was known as Shahjahanabad, the crown of the Moghul empire. Surrounded by massive walls with seven gates, it held the tombs of great emperors and glorious minarets. It also had a famous observatory, built by the Hindu maharaja Jai Singh II of Jaipur. Dominating it all was the towering Red Fort, the very image of Moghul splendor. Within the fort were streams and gardens, mosques and harems, the Golden Tower where emperors saluted the people, and a fabled throne room called the Diwan i Khas, or Hall of Public Audience. Its walls were white marble, its ceiling silver, and its floor divided by a sparkling stream. The Peacock Throne, ornamented with pearls, emeralds, and sapphires in their thousands, once stood in this hall; around the cornice of the building, in letters of gold,

A Bengal tiger pads through high grass and trees toward a water hole and his death. *Baghmars* (tiger killers) have positioned a spring bow poised to release a poison arrow when the animal steps on an attached cord near the water's edge. Fanny Parks drew this scene from the Rajmahal Hills, in northeast India.

ran the famous inscription: "If there be Paradise on earth, it is this, it is this."

By Fanny Parks's time, Paradise was no more than a shadow. The power center of India now lay in British Calcutta, and the aging Bahadur Shah II, the last of the Moghul emperors in Delhi, was a British pensioner. It was convenient to leave him as king of Delhi, but his kingdom was confined to the walls of his moldering palace, where he lived with uncounted servants, wives, children, and a personal bodyguard of 200, led by a British officer.

"See the Tajmahal, and then—see the Ruins of Delhi," Parks wrote. She had seen the Taj Mahal in all its unearthly perfection, only to discover to her outrage that her countrymen had hired a band to play on its marble terrace, while they danced quadrilles in front of the tomb. Now she saw Delhi. Thorough tourist that she was, she visited every monument and of course the palace, where she was invited to meet the shah's sister.

It proved to be a place of dark, dirty passages, of golden halls whose fountains were silent and whose marble floors were covered with black drainage water. Parks saw the sadness of vanished splendors. When British gossips accused her of visiting for the sake of presents from the princess, she was indignant: She had gone to the palace from curiosity, she said, and given the customary present of gold herself, receiving flowers in return. "In former times strings of pearls and valuable jewels were placed on the neck of departing visitors. When the Princess Hyat-ool-Nissa Begam in her fallen fortunes put the necklace of freshly-gathered white jasmine flowers over my head, I bowed with as much respect as if she had been the queen of the universe. Others may look upon these people with contempt, I cannot; look at what they are, at what they have been!"

When Fanny Parks caught a fever in Delhi, she headed for the hills. She was in a vanguard. In the early part of the century, the British had begun to expand their holdings into high country: Simla at the edge of the Himalayas in the northwest, Darjeeling in the northeast, and the Nilgiri Hills in the south. These places, with their splendid scenery, cool, bracing air, and small Indian populations, were natural retreats. If many people blamed tropical illness on the unhealthy air of the plains, the hills were thought to bring health. By the 1820s sanitariums for the sick were there. Within a few years people were building holiday houses as well, and within a few decades the settlements were developing into hill stations, where the British could spend the summer and live in splendid isolation from the vast country they governed.

Parks's first destination was the Himalayan foothills to the north. The trip by palanquin, buggy, pony back, and *jampan* (a covered armchair carried by eight men) could take weeks in her day, before the roads were built. But the trek was worth it. The scenery recalled Switzerland, and Parks rejoiced in the mountain air. "The delicious air, so pure, so bracing, so unlike any air I had breathed for fifteen years," she wrote. "I fancied the lurking fever crept out of my body as I breathed the mountain air."

As the elevation grew higher, the plants of remembered childhood appeared: There were oak trees covered with moss and ivy; and raspberry, clematis, woodbine, and rhododendron. There were even stinging nettles. But at the same time, tigers and elephants hid in the forests, and the birds were spectacular. There were golden eagles and black eagles, red pheasants and blue pheasants, bush quail and rock quail, and the wild chickens of the forest.

Then there were the people who lived in the high country. Parks was surrounded by friends from all over. She trekked with them, picnicked with them, helped one supervise the building of a new house with a beautiful view. It might have stood on land whose rights had been purchased from tribespeople, and they, too, were fascinating to Parks: She found hill tribes, such as the Gurkhas, much more attractive than the poor of the plains. "I never meet a hardy, active little Gurkha, with a countenance like a Tartar, and his *kookree* [a curved knife] at his side, but I feel respect for him," she commented. Gurkha women, Parks

added, "acted with the natural courage inherent in us all, never having been taught that it was pretty and interesting to be sweet, timid creatures!"

Riding was dangerous along those mountain edges—"a pathway three feet in width . . . is a handsome road in the Hills." On the other hand, as Parks discovered, the British were already busy re-creating little English spas. She could not help noticing how well people there looked: "The children! it is charming to see their rosy faces; they look as well and as strong as any children in England." In a bazaar she found everything from foie gras to truffled woodcock, from champagne to Chinese books.

Little Englands were developing everywhere in India. Still, Fanny Parks, lover of the sublime and of the picturesque, did not seem to mind. In fact, she seemed perfectly able to balance the British world within which she somewhat eccentrically fitted and the Indian one whose romance she adored. She spent the rest of her time in India traveling in style, entertaining, and taking notes, always returning with pleasure to Charles in Allahabad. She wrote of one homecoming from a boat: "There is the Fort and the great Masjid, and the old peepul-tree, and the mem sahiba's home, and the chabutara [terrace] on the bank of the river, which is crowded with friends on the look out for the pilgrim, and ready to hail her return with the greatest pleasure."

It was clear that India was the high point of Fanny Parks's life. "Do not think of quitting India," wrote a friend of Fanny's, "it is a country far preferable to the cold climate, and still colder hearts of Europe." But ultimately Fanny had to leave, returning reluctantly to England in 1845, when Charles fell ill. Once home, she occupied herself by editing her journal into a book called *Wanderings of a Pilgrim in Search of the Picturesque*. It was published in 1850. In its author's typically high-flown cross-cultural style, the book was dedicated to her "beloved mother," but it opened with an invocation to Ganesha, the elephant-headed Hindu god who is the remover of obstacles, invoked at the outset of any enterprise.

Discovering the Wonders of India

"It is my ambition to know India better than any other European ever knew it," declared Sir William Jones on his way to Calcutta in 1783. One of the first British intellectuals to develop a keen appreciation of the subcontinent, Jones was a tireless promoter of Indian scholarship. In 1784 he founded the Asiatic Society in Calcutta. Characteristic of the era's wide-ranging spirit of inquiry, it would be, he said, devoted to the study of the "history, arts, sciences and literature of Asia." Before long, members of Jones's society were joined in India by like-minded individuals interested in broadening their knowledge of the world around them.

English landscape artists Thomas and William Daniell and portrait painters such as James Wales and George Chinnery traveled to India and were captivated by it. They marveled at its breathtaking landscapes, massive ancient monuments, and picturesque scenes of daily life—a culture rich in inspiration.

India's spectacular variety of plant and animal life especially attracted naturalists. Professionals foraged for specimens in the wild, and amateurs acquired vast collections—often hiring Indian artists to render their prized items.

Surveyors general, such as Colonel Colin MacKenzie, provided the world with its first maps and measurements of the subcontinent. One of MacKenzie's successors, George Everest, began the work that would determine the height of the Himalayan peaks; the earth's highest mountain there bears his name.

A gifted linguist, Sir William Jones, who sat on the Supreme Court in Calcutta, boasted, "I can now read . . . Sanskrit . . . with so much ease that native lawyers can never impose upon the courts in which I sit." A statue of the Hindu god Ganesha graces his desk.

A watercolor by artist William Daniell portrays William
and his uncle, Thomas, in Bihar during one of their
expeditions. William examines the Bijaigarh hill fort
through a telescope while Thomas sits drawing the site,
shaded by attendants. The Daniells often included
themselves in their compositions.

Visitors gather at a magnificent waterfall known as Dhuan Kund, or Pool of Smoke, in the north of India. In his journal, Thomas Daniell described how the devotees would place their tents close to the water and to each other, enabling them to "form a little society" and "mingle somewhat of cheerfulness with their devotion."

Magnificent Landscapes

Hearing tales of fortunes to be made in far-off India, landscape painter Thomas Daniell requested permission from the East India Company to travel to Calcutta. Arriving in 1786 with his nephew William as his assistant, Daniell began making engravings of public buildings, which he sold to wealthy British residents.

Drawn by what lay outside of Calcutta, the Daniells used their profits to finance an expedition into the Indian countryside. Heading north, by river and often on foot, they and a small contingent of attendants hauled equipment and supplies for what became a three-year journey.

They trekked to ancient sacred cities and to the Taj Mahal, to ruins of Buddhist and Hindu temples, and even to the foothills of the Himalayas. Entranced by the unfamiliar landscape, they sketched it all; the better, as Thomas said, to "transport back picturesque beauties of these favored regions."

Though they usually slept in tents, they sometimes found more-interesting accommodations. The pair once happened upon an abandoned, dilapidated palace, and it provided, as William wrote, a "satisfactory abode" for several days.

Periodic art sales enabled the Daniells to finance other trips. Traveling south, they painted spectacular scenes from Madras to Cape Comorin, at India's southern tip. During their final trek west to Bombay, they explored the massive hand-carved rock caves that were to astonish them and many of their contemporaries.

The Daniells left India for good in 1793. But with the publication of *Oriental Scenery*, their collection of 144 aquatints, they brought part of India home to England and forever shaped the British perception of this distant land.

Rock Temples

"Stupendous work," wrote British artist James Wales in 1792 of his first view of the Buddhist rock cave temple at Karli. Carved in the face of the Western Ghats, the steep hills separating the coastal plain and the central plateau southeast of Bombay, the temple dated from the first century AD. Unlike anything Wales had ever seen before, Karli, along with other cave complexes in the area, had been hollowed out of the rock by Buddhists, Hindus, and Jains as places of worship and monastic residence through the ages.

James Wales had arrived in Bombay the previous year, intrigued by sketches he had seen of a rock temple on the island of Elephanta. The images inspired Wales to visit the great cave there with its high, pillared hall, housing a towering three-headed bust of the Hindu gods Brahma, Vishnu, and Shiva. Working as both artist and amateur archaeologist, he explored Elephanta and Karli, as well as caves on nearby Salsette Island. Wales took meticulous measurements, copied inscriptions, and sketched the ornate interiors of the caves.

Though he had planned to publish his work on these antiquities, Wales reportedly "fell victim to the putrid air inhaled in the caves" and died in 1795. Thomas Daniell, who had visited the caves with Wales, made aquatints from his friend's drawings and later published them.

Following Wales's lead, artist Henry Salt visited Karli in 1804. A companion wrote later of their awe at coming upon the temple: "The entrance to the temple was through a very lofty gateway, I should suppose about one hundred feet high, covered with carved work to the summit." So much earth and rock had been gouged by hand, then carved with great delicacy, all with rudimentary tools, that the explorers were overwhelmed by the devotion of the followers of the ancient faith.

To give a sense of its enormous scale, Henry Salt placed a visitor next to a stone pillar in his depiction of the Buddhist temple at Karli *(right)*. The temple's cavernous interior *(far right)*, with the carved arches of its ceiling and cylindrical rock shrine called a stupa, was engraved by Thomas Daniell after James Wales's original drawing.

CHAPTER THREE

Dominion and Uprising

Draped in ceremonial robes of scarlet and white, Governor General Richard Wellesley rests his hand atop a treaty made with the nizam of Hyderabad. Two more treaties, including one for the partition of Mysore, lie nearby. Through a combination of warfare and iron diplomacy, Wellesley expanded British possessions in India, transforming Britain into an imperial power.

I n Calcutta, on June 8, 1798, Governor General Richard Wellesley sat down to read a local newspaper and found his attention riveted by a startling news item. It was the reprint of a proclamation issued by the French governor general of Mauritius, an island in the Indian Ocean. Evidently posted throughout the island with little fear that its contents would reach British eyes, the proclamation stated that Tipu Sultan, ruler of India's southern state of Mysore, had sent envoys to Mauritius, hoping to form a defensive and offensive alliance. Having no troops to spare, the French governor general was asking instead for volunteers to join Mysore's army. Tipu waited only for French assistance "to declare war against the English, whom he ardently desires to expel from India."

Galvanized into action, Wellesley dispatched a copy of the proclamation and a letter to Major General George Harris, the military commander at Fort St. George and acting governor of the Madras presidency. In his letter, Wellesley suggested that the general, whose presidency was the closest to Mysore, should quietly but immediately begin preparations for war.

Thirty-seven-year-old Richard Wellesley, second earl of Mornington, had arrived on the subcontinent only six weeks before. The offspring of Anglo-Irish nobility and the eldest of five sons, Wellesley had been groomed to rule. Although the ancestral estates were mortgaged to the hilt, no expense had been spared on his education. He was an accomplished scholar and skilled orator, who, as a rising young politician, enjoyed the friendship of the prime minister, William Pitt, and the foreign secretary, William Grenville. Wellesley was fiercely ambitious, greedy not so much for money as for power and renown.

Richard Wellesley paid a high price for becoming British India's governor general. He left behind his children and his beloved wife, Hyacinthe. Hyacinthe returned that love—but she refused to go to India, which would have meant leaving her children in England or subjecting them to the subcontinent's dangers. During the long voyage to his new post, Richard wrote to her: "The ship reminds me of our horrible separation and I remember that I am travelling yet further away from all that is dearest to me on earth."

Still Wellesley believed India would be the stage on which to lay the foundations of a brilliant career. And the first step would be dealing with the threat posed by Mysore and France. The powerful state of Mysore had been a thorn in Britain's side ever since Muslim soldier Haidar Ali had overthrown the Hindu ruling house almost 40 years before. Haidar Ali and his son and successor, Tipu Sultan, were ambitious rulers who had fought to expand their territory. There had already been three Anglo-Mysore wars. In the third conflict, which ended in 1792, Tipu had been forced by a joint alliance of the British, the nizam of Hyderabad (the Muslim ruler to Mysore's north), and the Marathas (a loose confederation of Hindu rulers in central India and on the northwest coast) to sign a treaty giving up large tracts of land to the three allies, to pay war reparations, and to surrender two young sons as hostages until the terms of the treaty had been met.

The British had beaten the man they called the Tiger of Mysore, but he had not been vanquished. Educated in world politics, science, theology, and literature, and conversant in several languages, Tipu was a fierce and determined ruler who could be generous to loyal subjects

A tiger pounces on an East India Company officer in this macabre life-size curio once belonging to Tipu Sultan. A barrel organ inside the beast could be cranked to emit growls and shrieks.

Beneath a golden canopy topped with a bird of paradise, Tipu Sultan sits on an octagonal throne supported by a snarling tiger and adorned with eight small bejeweled tiger heads. When British forces stormed Tipu's capital in 1799, they seized the throne as war spoils.

but ruthless with those who opposed him. He saw the British as dangerous and sought his own alliances with the Marathas and the nizam of Hyderabad—with little success. But revolutionary France had been at war with Britain since January 1793; the French could prove ready allies.

To Wellesley, a French strike into India seemed probable in mid-1798. Napoleon's army was on the move and less than a month after Wellesley had read the Mauritius proclamation, Napoleon invaded Egypt. The subcontinent could be next, and Wellesley prepared for war. But as the months passed, an invasion seemed less and less likely. And reports numbered the French volunteers arriving in Mysore as no more than 150. Still Wellesley considered Tipu Sultan "a desperate and treacherous enemy" with whom the British had to deal.

In March 1799 an allied force of British troops and soldiers of the nizam of Hyderabad attacked Seringapatam, Mysore's capital. The defenders were soon forced to retreat behind the walls of their ruler's citadel. For nearly a month the British laid siege to the citadel. Finally, Tipu asked General Harris for terms of surrender. Mysore's ruler, Harris replied, must give up more than half his kingdom; pay large war reparations; and offer four of his sons as hostages. A furious Tipu refused. It would be better, he exclaimed, "to die like a soldier than to live a miserable dependent on the infidels, in the list of their pensioned rajas."

At 1 p.m. on May 4, 1799, after three days of artillery bombardment of the citadel, the British stormed a breach in the walls. A fierce battle ensued as Indian swords met the charge of British bayonets. But the fortress soon fell. After a lengthy search, the victors found Tipu's lifeless body in a pile of dead and dying. The British laid the fallen leader's body in a palanquin and carried it back to the palace. At General Harris's orders, the Tiger of Mysore would be given a state funeral.

The conquerors turned to dividing up the spoils. Fabulous jewels, bars of gold, silver plates, rich furniture, silk, china, and even books were snatched up. The greatest prize, though, was Mysore itself. The British pensioned off Tipu's sons to the Carnatic coast, and in their stead set a British puppet, the five-year-old heir of the dynasty Haidar Ali had displaced. He would nominally rule over a much reduced kingdom. The company annexed almost half of Mysore outright, sharing the gains with the nizam. The British portion served crucially to link its east-coast possessions around Madras to the Malabar Coast in the west. After Mysore's fall Wellesley wrote the company directors: "No particular comment is required from me to illustrate the numerous advantages which cannot fail to flow from [this] brilliant and decisive achievement."

Mysore would be just the beginning for Wellesley, whose actions and policies would accelerate the process of transforming the British into imperial rulers during the 19th century. Relations between the British and the Indians would also be changed. Social interactions would become more restricted, and the policy of excluding Indians from high government positions, begun under Governor General Charles Cornwallis in the 1780s, would worsen.

Attitudes toward Indian cultures and beliefs would change as well. British policy would shift from respect for Hindu and Muslim customs and ideology to an Anglicization of India. Christian missionaries would flock to the subcontinent, determined to convert the "heathen" Hindus and Muslims. Some Indians would seek to develop a way of life that blended East and West, walking an uneasy path between the two.

Seeking to Westernize India, the British would often ignore the effects their changes wrought on the people they ruled. Many

A 17th-century Englishman wears silk drawstring trousers modeled after the Indian *paijama*, with matching coat and European shoes, while exploring the countryside with a young companion.

Bringing India Home

Since their arrival in the 17th century, the British had been bringing changes to India, a process that would intensify during the 19th century. However, India in turn influenced the Britons, who brought back to England not only new ideas in dress, architecture, and food, but changes in language as well.

Many 17th-century East India Company officials and other British visitors adopted Indian dress for comfort. One such article of clothing was the *paijama,* loose silk or cotton drawstring trousers worn by Indian men and women. Britons brought the trousers home, inspiring 19th-century Western designers to fashion lounge- and sleepwear known as pajamas.

Indian architecture made its way to England through the aquatints of Thomas Daniell and his nephew William, published in Britain and India in the late 18th and early 19th centuries. Inspired by the Daniells' work, a retired Bengal civil servant constructed a home, called Sezincote, replete with domes, arches, pavilions, and minarets in the Cotswold Hills of southwest-central England. At his seaside retreat in Brighton, the Prince of Wales (later King George IV) built stables and a riding house influenced by Indian architecture and, be-ginning in 1805, proceeded to transform a cottage into a Moghul's palace. Not everyone appreciated the design, with its many small onion domes. One 19th-century visitor quipped, "The dome of St. Paul's must have come to Brighton and pupped."

Following on the heels of the architectural craze came a taste for Indian food. Any sauced dish cooked in the Indian style came to be called a curry—a possible corruption of a South Indian word for sauce, *kari.* The combination of spices used in such dishes was known as curry powder. Isabella Beeton, doyenne of English cookery, and others published recipes for curry pow-

Onion domes and minarets inspired by the Taj Mahal crown the Royal Pavilion at Brighton, offering visitors to the south coast of England the illusion of faraway India.

der, which included such spices as coriander seed, turmeric, cinnamon, cayenne pepper, and fenugreek seed. One popular curried dish was kedgeree, adapted from *khichri*, which was made with rice, lentils, and butter. The Anglo version contained rice, fish, and chopped hard-boiled egg and became a staple of the English manor-house breakfast.

The collection of art from Britain's 250 years in India culminated in the Indian section of London's Great Exhibition of 1851. Queen Victoria admired "the splendid jewels and shawls, embroideries, silver bedsteads, [and] ivory chairs" on display and commented that it was "quite something new for the generality of people." The London *Times* called the exhibit, which was mounted by the East India Company, "one of the most complete, splendid, and interesting collections in Hyde Park, instructive in a great variety of ways, and the merit of which cannot be too highly praised."

Tipu Sultan was the inspiration for the name of this curry powder. *Saib* was a misspelling of *sahib*, or master, a term of respect that was used for both Indians and Europeans.

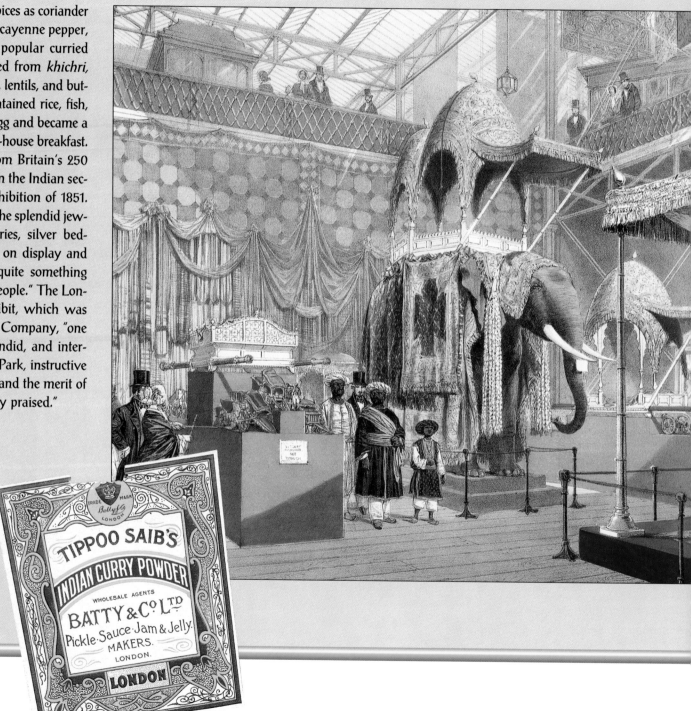

A silk-draped stuffed elephant with an ivory and gold-silk howdah, or covered seat, dominated the Great Exhibition's Indian section.

Indians would come to feel that their most sacred beliefs and rights were threatened. The result would be a terrifying explosion of violence.

"The manner in which I have conducted this war has been received with exaltations," Wellesley wrote to Foreign Secretary Grenville after Tipu's defeat. "You will gain much credit by conferring some high and brilliant honour upon me immediately."

Though taken aback by the presumption, Wellesley's friends in Britain arranged for him to be made a marquess and given a large monetary gift. The marquisate was an Irish title, like the one Wellesley already held. But an Irish title was inferior to an English title, and Wellesley had expected to receive the latter. Overwrought, he chose to regard the offer as a snub. "I cannot describe my anguish of mind," he complained to the prime minister. To Hyacinthe he wrote even more passionately, "If I die, let the world know they have caused my death."

If Wellesley could not get the honor he wanted from England, he made sure he received it in India. He surrounded himself with a large entourage of splendidly dressed retainers and servants and performed official acts with great ceremony. The result was a show of pomp and circumstance the likes of which British India had never seen.

Building projects provided another opportunity for displaying magnificence. Wellesley replaced the old Government House with a structure that occupied a whole block. It had a domed central section for state apartments and four domestic wings linked to it by curving corridors. Wellesley began construction on a country residence at Barrackpore, 14 miles away. When finished, it would be a palace complete with theater, indoor riding arena, and zoo.

Although Wellesley's justification for such extravagance

was a need to impress his Indian subjects, few of them actually entered these buildings. Unlike the British of only a few years before, Wellesley did not mix easily with Indians, who were increasingly isolated from the seat of power. Noting the change, one old India hand deplored the fact that the Indian population "are excluded from all posts of great respectability or emolument, and are treated in society with mortifying hauteur and reserve."

While infusing the governorship with ever more status, Wellesley was also enlarging his dominions. Wellesley most often sought expansion by iron diplomacy rather than open war. The vehicle of expansion was a system of forced alliances—known as subsidiary alliances—used to secure the compliance of nominally independent states. By this arrangement, the British stationed military forces in the lands of Indian rulers as "protection" against their Indian enemies. The rulers had to pay for the British soldiers, who, once in place, also enforced British dominion. If cash payments were not forthcoming, the company took land instead.

Though previous governors general had used the alliance system, Wellesley made more aggressive use of it than his predecessors. He pressured the nizam of Hyderabad into giving up the cotton-rich region of Berar. The young heir to the Carnatic states was simply disinherited when he rejected Wellesley's terms, and a company puppet was installed in his stead. The entire southeastern state of Tanjore was absorbed, as was the port of Surat, where Sir Thomas Roe had arrived in India some 185 years before.

In December 1801 Wellesley ratified a treaty with the nawab of Oudh. Under its terms, the nawab would surrender the fertile and productive regions of western Doab and Rohilkhand outright, while retaining nominal rule over the rest of his territory. To finalize details, Wellesley traveled to Lucknow, the nawab's seat of government. He started up the Ganges from Calcutta in a flotilla of green-and-gold boats, rowed by scarlet-liveried oarsmen. Horses often kept pace with the fleet on the riverbank, so the British could go riding when they felt the need for exercise. Sometimes the younger officers went tiger hunting.

For the final stage, overland, Wellesley was escorted by one cavalry and two infantry regiments and a couple of troops of dragoons, which together with camp followers amounted to an escort of more than 20,000 people. In Lucknow, Wellesley and the nawab, riding atop an elephant, led a procession through the streets. Buildings along the route had been freshly painted, and some were adorned with rich and varied silks. Musicians and dancers performed on rooftops. Wellesley, wrote one English observer, threw rupees to the watching crowds "in the true style of Eastern pomp." Then began a round of dinner parties, firework displays, and a ball. "I am received in all countries here like a Tutelary Deity—" Wellesley wrote to his wife; "it is very flattering."

Wellesley had no authority for his pell-mell system of acquisition; the India Act of 1784 had specified that "to pursue schemes of conquest and extension of dominion in India, are measures repugnant to the wish, the honour, and the policy of this nation."

"I am received in all countries here like a Tutelary Deity—it is very flattering."

The nawab of Oudh gestures to Lord Wellesley as they watch an elephant fight that has been staged for the governor general's entertainment. Wellesley pressured the once-powerful ruler to abdicate, and when the nawab reneged on an agreement to do so, the governor general forced him to sign a treaty ceding Britain half the state of Oudh.

As for the East India Company's directors, whose interests Wellesley was supposed to represent, they were horrified by his actions, seeing in each annexation only enhanced responsibilities and shrunken profits. But the directors were in London, half a world away.

There was one force in India that could threaten British hegemony—the Marathas. These independent Hindu rulers shared between them the arid uplands of the Deccan in south-central India. Their power stretched north all the way to Delhi, where the Moghul emperor eked out a confined existence under their protection. Marathas were fierce fighters, well trained and equipped, with great loyalty to their individual leaders. Fortunately for Wellesley's ambitions, those rulers had long since fallen out. The Marathas

Visiting dignitaries pass beneath a triumphal arch to enter Hyderabad's British residency, whose grand architecture was modeled after Lord Wellesley's Government House in Calcutta. The British resident at Hyderabad justified such an extravagant display of grandeur by claiming "authority must either be seen or it must be felt."

had been fighting among themselves for the last two decades.

Even though he had received specific instructions from the directors in London not "to involve us in the endless and turbulent distractions of the Marathas," Wellesley played one faction off against another to gain land and control. In 1803 an outbreak of hostilities developed into a two-year running war. The British forces waged various campaigns against the formidable Maratha armies, eventually emerging triumphant.

When news of the war reached the East India Company

directors, they formally censured Wellesley for overexpenditure and disobeying orders. The governor general resigned and sailed home in August 1805. He was subsequently brought before Parliament to answer charges of abuse of office, but a vote for censure was defeated. He went on to enjoy a distinguished career as ambassador to Spain, foreign secretary, and lord lieutenant of Ireland. Wellesley died in 1842 at age 82.

Richard Wellesley had had many grand ideas for British India, among them establishing a university in Calcutta to teach newly arrived company servants the local languages and legal systems. These subjects and others would prepare the young Britons for their new positions and help "to establish the British Empire in India on the solid foundations of ability, integrity, virtue, and religion." Wellesley's vision was considerably reduced in scope by the company directors, but it did come to partial fruition with the foundation of Fort William College in late 1800.

Baptist missionary William Carey agreed with Wellesley's aims and became a teacher at the college in 1801. More than one person was shocked by Carey's appointment, however. In the early 19th century, the company still denied Christian missionaries the licenses all Europeans living in British India were required to obtain, fearing the quest for converts could only unsettle the Hindu and Muslim populations. But unofficially, British authorities such as Wellesley supported the missionaries' efforts.

Carey had been born the son of a weaver in the English Midlands in 1761. Although he had little formal education, he had a talent for languages, teaching himself Greek while still a young man. After training as a shoemaker, he took a job as a village schoolmaster, during which time he became a Baptist. A reading of the voyages of Captain James Cook interested him in the idea of spreading the Gospel abroad. In June 1793 he and fellow missionary John Thomas, who had already spent time preaching in Bengal, set out for India under the auspices of the Baptist Missionary Society. A reluctant Dorothy Carey, William's wife, went as well, along with their four small children.

Having no British licenses, the party booked passage on a Danish ship and arrived in Bengal in November 1793. As the ship lay at anchor at the mouth of the Hooghly River, Thomas and Carey went ashore to the nearest marketplace, where Thomas began preaching. The courteous attention displayed by the Indians inspired Carey with hope for the success of the mission.

By a stroke of good fortune, Thomas and Carey got jobs six months after their arrival in India, managing neighboring indigo factories 300 miles upstream. Though the area contained tigers, snakes, and crocodiles, Carey claimed to be unconcerned. Tigers usually attacked cattle rather than people, he wrote. "Crocodiles no man minds: I have one in a pond about ten yards from my door, yet sleep with the door open every night."

His new job suited William Carey well. The salary proved generous, home was a pleasant two-story brick house, and as an indigo factory manager, he was able to get a license to work and live in British India. The work demands kept him busy for only three months of the year, when the indigo was processed, leaving him plenty of time to learn Indian languages, the essential tools for carrying out his mission. Carey had begun his studies of Bengali on the ship with Thomas and continued them with Ram Basu, a munshi, or language tutor. Within a year of his arrival in India, Carey was preaching in Bengali.

From the study of Bengali, Carey turned to the classical language of Sanskrit. He began writing a grammar of the language in English and preparing a dictionary in Bengali, Sanskrit, and English. He and Ram Basu worked on translating the Christian Bible into Bengali. He also set up a school for Indian boys, teaching them Persian and Sanskrit, the Bible, and science and mathematics. Carey, and especially Thomas, who was a doctor, also tried to help the sick and injured. In the poor villages where there was little access to medical care, Thomas's care could be invaluable.

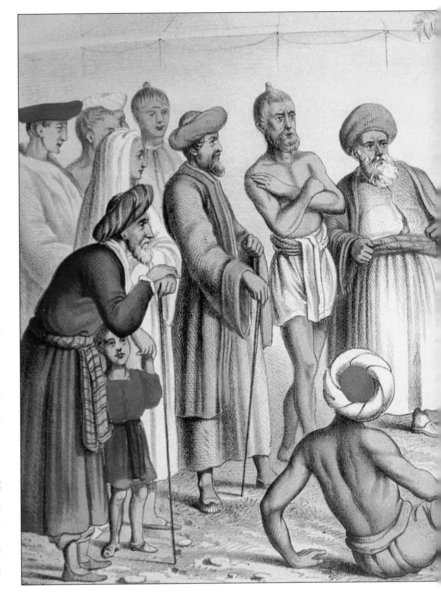

In his first seven years in India, Carey worked to support his family and his mission and continued to study, teach, translate, and preach. At first, his 90 factory employees seemed a ready-made congregation, ripe for conversion. But they proved a more difficult audience than he had expected. The day before the indigo factory began production, workers approached Carey about making an offering to the goddess Kali. The missionary lectured them, as he had other Indians, on "the folly and wickedness of

Idolatry." The people listened politely and then left—to sacrifice a lamb to the goddess on his behalf.

Carey tried preaching elsewhere. Traveling by small boat from village to village, he and Thomas spoke about Christianity to anyone who would listen. Yet he failed to make any conversions at all among the Indians in those first years.

In October 1799 a party of eight Baptist missionaries and their families arrived from England. Having had some problems with the British officials, the group settled in Serampore, a small Danish settlement 15 miles north of Calcutta, where the Careys soon joined them. Pooling resources, the missionaries bought some property with several buildings. One would be used for a chapel and the others for residential and business needs. Of primary importance was setting up a printing press to publish Carey's translations and other publications. Carey was determined to produce inexpensive copies of the Christian Bible for wide dissemination.

Two of the new arrivals, Joshua and Hannah Marshman, opened a boarding school for Europeans, offering lessons in Latin, Greek, Hebrew, Persian, and Sanskrit. It was soon doing well.

Earnings from the school and the press were plowed back into the mission to fund enterprises such as a free school for Bengali boys. The first Indian convert was baptized in December 1800.

Carey's personal star rose when his Bengali translation of the New Testament came out in 1801. Despite the company's official disapproval of mission work, Carey sent a copy of it to Governor General Wellesley. From a prior encounter in Calcutta with a company chaplain, Carey had discovered that

A Protestant missionary expounds on Christian doctrine, his words translated for listeners by the Indian assistant beside him *(above)*. With the help of munshis and pandits, missionaries such as Baptist William Carey learned to speak and read modern and classical Indian languages. At right, Carey is shown working with pandit Mrityunjay.

Wellesley knew of the missionaries' activities and had no problems with them. The chaplain was certain, Carey wrote, "we might have preached anywhere in the town."

As it happened, the governor general needed linguists for Fort William College. Few Anglo-Indians, however, were qualified to teach the languages of India, and though the college would employ Indian pandits—learned Brahmans—and munshis, they would not be hired for the higher positions of teacher and professor. A month after the New Testament translation, Wellesley gave his approval to hire Carey to teach Bengali and Sanskrit. Carey's first task was producing materials in Bengali for his students. Most written material in Bengali was in verse; Carey needed prose. Ram Basu came to Carey's aid, writing a history of one of the Bengali kings, "the first prose book ever written in the Bengali language." He also translated some Sanskrit fables. Carey worked on his grammar of Sanskrit and the trilingual dictionary he had begun years before.

In a letter written to a friend in 1806, Carey described a typical day in Calcutta. He rose at 5:45 a.m. and read a chapter of the Bible in Hebrew. Before breakfast at 7:00, there was time for prayers and for a Persian reading with a munshi, as well as for perusing some biblical verses in Hindustani. After breakfast, he settled down with a pandit to work on translating the Ramayana, a great Sanskrit epic, into English. At 10 o'clock he took up his teaching duties, which continued into the early afternoon. Then he went through the proofs of a Bengali version of the Old Testament until dinner, which he took in the late afternoon.

In the evening, he labored on a translation of the Christian Gospels into Sanskrit, took lessons in the Telugu language from another pandit, and wrote and preached a sermon to followers. That left time before bed for readings from the Bible in Greek—and, of course, for writing the letter. "I have never more time in a day than this, though the exercises vary," he concluded.

PERILOUS JOURNEYS

Traveling in India during the early 19th century could be a dangerous undertaking for merchants and pilgrims, for highway murders and robberies were common in the northern heartland. The British blamed many of these crimes on a practice called thuggee. According to British authorities, robbers known as thugs waylaid travelers, then strangled and robbed them *(below)* as part of a professed allegiance to the Hindu goddess of destruction, Kali.

William Sleeman *(left)*, an East India Company military officer stationed during the 1820s in Jubbulpore, in north-central India, sought to eradicate thuggee. He interviewed thug-group members and compiled their genealogies to show that membership was hereditary. In 1836 an act was passed allowing authorities to convict a person for membership in a thug gang—an easier charge to prove than murder.

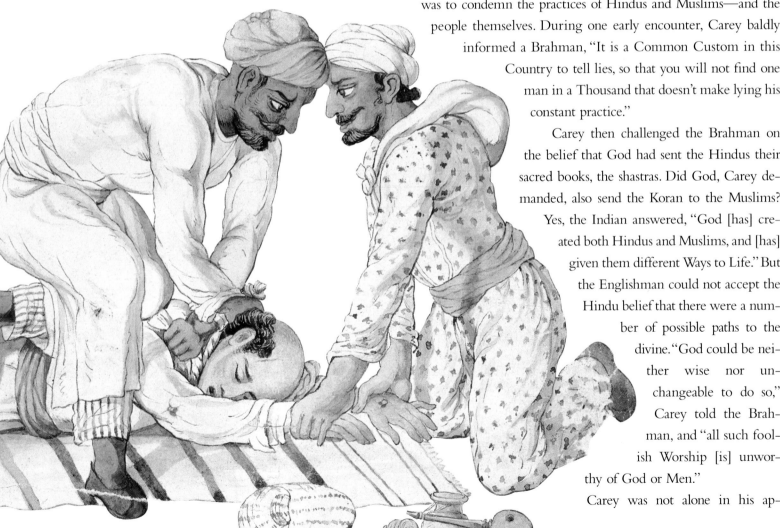

On weekends he traveled by boat to Serampore, where the mission's many activities were flourishing. The printing operation was by now producing and selling its own type and printer's ink, and in time it also had a paper mill to supply its needs. Soon enough money was coming in to finance mission stations elsewhere in Bengal. A small army of Indian pandits was employed for the great work of biblical translation.

The preaching continued as well. Carey and other missionaries found that not everyone appreciated the Christians' attempts at conversion, particularly in the early years when the approach was to condemn the practices of Hindus and Muslims—and the people themselves. During one early encounter, Carey baldly informed a Brahman, "It is a Common Custom in this Country to tell lies, so that you will not find one man in a Thousand that doesn't make lying his constant practice."

Carey then challenged the Brahman on the belief that God had sent the Hindus their sacred books, the shastras. Did God, Carey demanded, also send the Koran to the Muslims? Yes, the Indian answered, "God [has] created both Hindus and Muslims, and [has] given them different Ways to Life." But the Englishman could not accept the Hindu belief that there were a number of possible paths to the divine. "God could be neither wise nor unchangeable to do so," Carey told the Brahman, and "all such foolish Worship [is] unworthy of God or Men."

Carey was not alone in his approach. William Ward, who ran the printing plant, called the Islamic prophet Muhammad a murderer and adulterer during an argument with one Muslim. These attacks were bound to cause trouble—and did. In Serampore, Brahmans came to dispute the missionaries' teachings, and the Baptists found themselves assaulted, in Carey's words, "with all the insulting language that malice could invent." Some Baptists, Carey among them, eventually learned that the Indian people responded better to a discussion of Christianity's positive attributes rather than disparagement of Hinduism or Islam.

Further trouble for the missionaries and the British arose in 1806, in the distant town of Vellore, 80 miles west of Madras. The most immediate cause would later be attributed to orders at the fort requiring the Indians to remove the marks on their foreheads that identified the sect to which they belonged and, instead of turbans, wear European hats, which incorporated leather and feathers. The British ignored the fact that both orders challenged Hindu beliefs. In the local uprising that followed, sepoys killed 129 Europeans and loyalist sepoys before the British took back the fort, killing 350 Indians in turn.

Some people blamed the incident on the unsettling effects of missionary activity. Old company hands, who had never liked what they saw as the missionaries' meddling in Indian affairs, spoke out against the activities. For a short time after Vellore, acting governor general Sir George Barlow curtailed missionary activities. Some restrictions were soon eased, though Barlow continued to prohibit the circulation of tracts railing against Hinduism and Islam, open-air preaching, and sending Indian converts to proselytize outside Serampore.

Another blow would follow six years later. On the night

Resplendent in his dress uniform, Tom Raw attempts to impress Calcutta society at a Government House ball, but as he chats with an Armenian couple he clumsily gashes a dancer's gown with his sword and then steps on and tears the dress's hem *(far right)*.

As the riverboat carries him to his first post, Tom prefers napping to admiring the scenery that has captivated his fellow traveler *(above)*. At right, a tiger leaps on the hapless Tom's howdah during a hunt, sending the terrified griffin scrambling to escape. A more seasoned companion on a neighboring elephant dispatches the beast.

Griffins and the Town of Kabob

Two longtime residents of India, Sir Charles D'Oyly and Captain George Atkinson, poked fun at the pretensions of their countrymen in India by writing books that satirized Anglo-Indian life. Both writers knew India well. D'Oyly, who was born in Calcutta but educated in England, served the British East India Company in a variety of posts, from court clerk to opium customs collector. He wrote and illustrated *Tom Raw, the Griffin*, an 1828 publication that lampooned the career of a bumbling cadet in the British East India Company army. *Griffin* was slang for newcomer among the India service veterans, and Tom Raw, whose parents arrange a cadetship to get him out of a too-crowded family home, is a particularly inept newcomer to the subcontinent. Tom is befuddled by hookahs and Indian dancing girls and falls through the bottom of his palanquin "stern foremost" as he is being transported to his new post. Despite his blundering, the young cadet manages, purely by accident, to become a military hero and earn himself a promotion.

was described in one Serampore missive as "disgusting," bringing to mind "practices dishonourable to God." Carey and his Protestant colleagues insisted on wearing English clerical garb, even while recognizing that it was quite unsuitable for tropical climes. One complained of having to preach in woolen clothes that caused the papers in his pocket to be dyed black with sweat.

Indians might not have been listening to the missionaries, but British officials obviously were. In 1813 the clause barring missionaries from British India was dropped. A new clause stated it was Britain's duty to promote "religious and moral improvement" on the subcontinent. Many undoubtedly believed that Christianity was desperately needed in India. But they also hoped that newly converted Indians would help to secure British interests.

Carey would continue to work as a missionary until his death in June 1834. During his time in India, he made a significant contribution to Bengali and other Indian languages with prose books, dictionaries, grammars, and other publications. He opened schools for Indians and offered medical treatment to those in need. In 1820 he helped establish the Agricultural and Horticultural Society of India in hopes of improving Indian methods of farming. As a missionary, he could be insulting and dismissive of Indian religious beliefs and customs, but he devoted decades of his life to his adopted land. A few years before his death, he wrote to a friend, "My heart is wedded to India and though I am of little use, I feel pleasure in doing the little I can."

Most Christian converts, wrote Brahman reformer Rammohan Roy in 1820, had "been allured to change their faith by other attractions than by a conviction of the truth and reasonableness." Roy referred to the small monetary allowances and room and board the Baptists offered people who attended religious classes and to the jobs in the Serampore printing plant and paper mill given to converts. The missionaries stated that they offered such benefits because converts faced ostracism within their own communities and even the threat of violence. But to Roy it meant that Indians, especially poor ones, were being bribed to convert—an action this religious and social reformer found appalling.

One day in 1820 or 1821, Rammohan Roy left the residence of the Anglican

Hindu Brahman, scholar, and reformer Rammohan Roy played a major role in the intellectual life of early-19th-century India. His views on religion and culture sparked fierce debate among British missionaries and Hindu pandits, helping to elevate the public's political and social awareness.

bishop of Calcutta and climbed into his waiting carriage. He directed the driver to take him to the nearby home of his friend William Adam, who immediately invited his unexpected visitor inside. Roy agreed to have some refreshment but asked that Adam send his servants away before bringing any food or drink. Roy was afraid they would spread the news that he had lost caste if he were seen to eat in the home of a Christian. Repeatedly assailed by orthodox Hindus, Roy could not afford such talk.

Alone with Adam, Roy finally unburdened himself. He had accepted an invitation to the bishop's home, where the distinguished Brahman had listened incredulously as the clergyman tried to persuade him to declare himself a Christian. To sweeten the prospect, the Anglican assured his Hindu visitor that he would enjoy a "grand

British, he neither rejected nor accepted beliefs and customs outright. He sought the best of East and West, as he saw it, and tried to change what he thought of as wrong. It was a difficult road to walk, one which often alienated Indians and Britons alike. But he believed strongly, "If in doubt, consult your own conscience."

Born in 1772, Rammohan Roy came from a family of well-off Brahman landowners with a taste for learning. As a young man he studied Sanskrit, Arabic, and Persian and took an interest in Islam. At age 25 Roy moved to Calcutta and set himself up in business as a moneylender. Here several friendships blossomed with Indian and European intellectuals, and his studies expanded to include English, Latin, Hebrew, and Greek as well as Christianity.

Among his Calcutta friends was a young man

"If in doubt, consult your own conscience."

career," and "his name would descend to posterity as that of the modern Apostle of India."

Rammohan Roy angrily took his leave. He had spent his life studying Hinduism, Christianity, and other religions and had engaged in serious public debate about them—often at great personal cost. Yet this Englishman had actually had the effrontery to ask him to renounce his faith for the shallowest of reasons. "Not on the force of evidence, or for the love of truth, or for the satisfaction of his conscience, or for the benefit of his fellow-men," as Adam later recorded, "but for the sake of the honour and glory and fame it might bring him."

No worse an insult could have been offered to Rammohan Roy, because evidence, truth, conscience, and benefit to others were the forces that drove him. Living in a world both Indian and

named John Digby, a student at Fort William College. The two men shared common intellectual interests and spent their spare time reading and discussing the classics of Western literature. Given his British connections, Roy gravitated naturally to a job with the East India Company, which provided an excellent opportunity to improve his knowledge of English and gain a better understanding of European politics. For much of his company career, Roy worked with Digby at successive postings in Bengal. Starting out as a private secretary, he went on to serve as a court official and lastly as a diwan, or assistant to the collector. In the early 19th century, this was the highest position to which an Indian could aspire in company service, no matter how qualified.

Even before working for the company, Roy had been building up his real-estate holdings, and by 1815 these were substan-

1835 English replaced Persian as the language of official documents and the law courts. Funds for education were increased, and schools teaching English spread around the country.

During the next two decades, roads and railways were built across the subcontinent and the telegraph was introduced. Further social reforms were implemented; legal obstacles preventing Hindu widows from remarrying were removed, and converts to Christianity could no longer be barred from collecting their inheritances. But, increasingly convinced they were acting in the Indians' best interests, British officials gave less and less thought to the dislocation that other changes they imposed on India caused or how they were perceived by a subject population.

James Broun Ramsay, the marquess of Dalhousie, who became governor general in 1848, brought more independent Hindu states under the company's direct rule, using the "doctrine of lapse." Under it, the company could claim the territory of any ruler who died without a direct heir, a more frequent occurrence after the British decided not to recognize adopted sons as legitimate heirs.

Dalhousie also decided to apply the doctrine to any state that was conspicuously misgoverned. Oudh fit into this category, in his view. Deprived of real power, its rulers had turned inward. The British resident in Lucknow reported of its last ruler that "he appears wholly to have resigned himself to debauchery, dissipation and low pursuits." So in February 1856, the British deposed the nawab, pensioning him off to exile on an estate near Calcutta.

The move caused deep resentment. Despite Wellesley's annexation of two of its wealthier provinces, Oudh had remained a loyal British ally. There was genuine shock that the British should have treated an ally in such a way. The annexation also had a powerful impact on the sepoys, for a disproportionate number came from the state. Tensions began to rise. Shut away in their increasingly secluded European quarters and cantonments, or military encampments, few Britons were aware of the mounting resentment in Indian society. In 1855, just before boarding his ship for

India, the company's newest governor general, Charles Canning, gave a speech far more prophetic than he could have known. "We must not forget that in the sky of India, serene as it is, a cloud may arise, at first no bigger than a man's hand but which growing bigger and bigger may at last threaten to overwhelm us with ruin."

Just a year later, Harriet Tytler and her family arrived in Delhi. Captain Robert Tytler, Harriet's husband, was serving with an Indian regiment that had just been posted to the city. They were stationed in a cantonment, three miles outside the city walls, and it was there that the Tytlers and their two youngest children had their quarters. Their older children had been sent to boarding schools in England.

The British assigned only Indian regiments, such as the one captained by Robert Tytler, to Delhi. Bahadur Shah II, the 80-year-old Moghul emperor known now as the king of Delhi, still lived there amid the faded splendors of the Red Fort, but his dynasty had in effect been given notice to quit. Dalhousie, impatient to be rid of this symbol of Indian rule, had let it be known that Bahadur Shah II would be the last of his line recognized as king.

Harriet Tytler passed the time in the cantonment uneventfully. There were the children to care for and the servants to supervise. Otherwise, little happened; the only outings were a morning ride and a drive in the cool of the evening, the sole visitors other officers' wives. Harriet was a second-generation Anglo-Indian, though she had been sent to England for her education's sake at age 11, in 1839. Her experience of her home country, where she lived with a strict and severe aunt, was not happy. So she was thrilled to return to India six years later, where in 1848 she married Robert, a widower with two young sons.

As the months passed in Delhi, the Tytlers became aware of a growing discontent among the Indian troops. Sepoys in Delhi, Harriet noted, "evinced some insubordination," afraid the British were trying to forcibly convert their Indian troops.

For many the fears were of long standing. During various

Tracks across the Subcontinent

Governor General Dalhousie wrote on the eve of his departure from India in 1856 that he had endeavored to harness to the subcontinent's "bullock-cart" civilization "three great engines of social improvement . . .: Railways, uniform Postage, and the Electric Telegraph." In addition to Dalhousie's list, the British also overhauled India's irrigation system. But these advancements were as much a means of increasing revenues and maintaining control as they were of improving the lot of the Indians.

As more land became available to them, the British set about repairing India's old canals and reservoirs. These improvements made their land more productive, which helped avert famine and generate more taxes. New projects followed: In the mid-1830s, a great dam was constructed across the Godavari River in southern India, and in the north, the Ganges Canal, more than 500 miles long, was completed in 1854.

The primary impetus for building roads and railways was to facilitate the movement of British troops. Yet roads and railroads also made travel easier, faster, and cheaper for nonmilitary travelers. In 1839 the hinterlands opened with the construction of the Grand Trunk Road, which connected Calcutta and Delhi, and later extended across

Stone lions crouch at the headworks of the Ganges Canal, which diverted water from the Ganges to drought-prone areas north of Delhi.

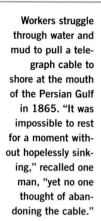

Punjab to Peshawar on the northwest frontier. The road bore "India's traffic for 1,500 miles," noted the writer Rudyard Kipling, "such a river of life as nowhere else exists in the world." And in 1853, the *Great Peninsular Railway* began to offer India's first railway passenger service.

Along with the rest of the world, India underwent revolutionary changes in communication in the 19th century. The first telegraph message within India was sent in 1851. By 1855 the telegraph system was linked with a new national postal service. A letter could be posted in India for the equivalent of about a penny, allowing communication with small villages as well as cities. Swift national communication helped the British maintain control of their empire. In 1857 the telegraph flashed news of the uprising, enabling British troops to respond

quickly. Telegraphic communication between Britain and India was opened in 1865.

Building canals and roads and laying railroad tracks and telegraph cables was grueling and dangerous work and many Indian and British lives were lost. But it provided an infrastructure that enabled Britain to maintain its grip on the subcontinent. And soon these improvements in travel and communication would help foster the sense of nation that would become so important for the Indians in the next century.

British soldiers fire on an Indian town from a steam-powered "gun-boat barge" in an October 1857 *Illustrated London News* picture that showed how such a vessel could have aided troops. Use of the barge had been proposed as early as 1849 but had been rejected.

A train travels a section of track called Agony Point, illustrating the loops engineers chose to use to cross mountains rather than blasting tunnels to go through them.

campaigns, the British had sent sepoy troops across the ocean to fight. Hindu troops could not cook for themselves and had to obtain food from lower castes or Muslims. When these sepoys returned home, they were shunned as unclean by other Hindus. British officials also supported the proselytizing of Christian missionaries and allowed officers to preach to their troops. And now the sepoys claimed they were being forced to pollute themselves with unclean animal fat. Why, the troops asked, would the British be doing all this if not to forcibly convert them to Christianity?

This most recent concern about animal fat involved the new Enfield rifles the British army had acquired. The new weapons used paper cartridges—one end of the cartridge containing a powder charge, the other containing a bullet. A soldier ripped open the cartridge's powder end—with either his teeth or his fingers—poured the powder down the gun barrel, then rammed the bullet down the barrel. To facilitate the loading of the bullet, the cartridge end was greased during manufacture. Ordnance officers in England decided that the best lubricants would be animal fats. But products from dead animals were forbidden to Hindus, and pork products, including pig fat, were forbidden to Muslims.

When the first cartridges reached India in January 1857, rumors about the grease circulated quickly among worried sepoys. As soon as they became aware of the problem, British commanders gave orders for the new cartridges to be withdrawn—but not before some ugly incidents occurred. One officer became so outraged at the men's refusal to accept the cartridges that he threatened, "I will take them to Rangoon or China, where they will suffer many privations, and all die." Level heads prevailed, and it was decided that the sepoys would be issued ungreased cartridges, which they would smear with beeswax and linseed oil. The authorities breathed a sigh of relief, thinking they had averted a crisis.

When some of the Delhi troops were ordered to nearby Ambala to learn to use the new rifles, Harriet Tytler hoped the Indian troops would see "we had no desire to destroy their caste and turn them into Christians." But word soon came back that the men continued to declare their dissatisfaction.

With an Indian servant riding on the back, a carriage rolls down the street of a British outpost, past thatch-roofed bungalows and a small, white-washed church. Harriet and Robert Tytler *(right)* lived in several little stations prior to Robert's assignment in Delhi.

Even more worrisome were reports that 85 sepoys at the garrison town of Meerut, just 40 miles northeast of Delhi, had refused to load the new cartridges. This was insubordination on a serious scale, and the Tytlers were pleased to learn that the British divisional commander was planning strong action. The sepoys were tried by a court-martial of Indian soldiers, presided over by a subahdar major—an Indian officer—in Robert Tytler's regiment, who had been called to Meerut. To Robert, the subahdar major vowed, "If I find these men guilty, I will give them the severest punishment in my power." As promised, the sepoys received a 10-year prison sentence. In front of the entire garrison, the offending soldiers were to be stripped of their uniforms and placed in shackles.

The punishment began on May 10. That evening, the Tytlers heard the sound of carriage wheels passing nearby and a bugle. Robert sent a servant to discover if the subahdar major had returned. The servant came back, telling Robert that it was only some sepoys from Meerut who had come to see friends. "My husband," Harriet noted, "thought it was a strange thing but never gave the matter any serious consideration."

The following morning, Harriet, now eight months pregnant with her fourth child, rose early as usual to bathe and feed the children. Robert and Harriet were just finishing their own breakfast when the Tytlers' tailor rushed in. "Sahib, Sahib, the fauj has come!" *Fauj* meant army, and from his agitated expression, the tailor was not referring to regular troops. Robert jumped to his feet. Confused, Harriet asked, "What is the matter?"

"Those fellows from Meerut have come over and I suppose are kicking up a row in the city," Robert replied, after calling for his boots and hat. "There is nothing to be frightened about, our men will be sent to coerce them and all will very soon be over."

Robert soon returned to let Harriet know that he had been detailed to guard a ferry over the Jumna River with two detachments of Indian troops. "Don't be frightened," he said before leaving again. But the Englishwoman could see something was seriously wrong. Artillery was being rushed down the main street, and people were racing about. Harriet saw the local judge's wife, hair spilling wildly over her shoulders, hurrying down the street in the opposite direction from the guns, a child in her arms.

Harriet soon received word that the camp commander had ordered all officers' wives to gather in a staff bungalow. From the bungalow, the families soon moved on to the Flagstaff Tower, a fortified outpost overlooking the city. In the turret they spent a long, hot day gradually piecing together the full dimensions of the conflict. The sepoys in Meerut had risen in revolt the previous evening and had started killing Europeans. The mutineers had then headed for Delhi, where they forced their way into the Red Fort to demand that the octogenarian Moghul emperor put himself at their head. In fear more than hope, he had accepted. Others in the city, including local sepoys, had rallied to the cause, and the killing of Europeans and Christians had ensued.

Harriet was desperate for news of her husband when, late in the afternoon, he arrived unexpectedly at the tower. All but about 30 or 40 of his troops had mutinied, running off toward the city, yelling, *"Prithiviraj ki jai!"* (Victory to the emperor!) Finding the women and children in the tower temporarily safe but with no access to food or water, Robert managed to persuade the camp commander to order an evacuation, with the promise that his remaining sepoys would help cover the retreat. So began a terrifying exodus, as the surviving officers and their families crowded into any available conveyance and set out through the outer suburbs for the safety of Ambala—and the nearest British regiments—more than 120 miles away.

Robert's remaining sepoys stayed with the British until they learned that a young British subaltern had blown up the magazine, injuring two sepoys assigned to guard it. Believing themselves betrayed, the rest of the sepoys deserted, but they left the British officers and families unharmed. As the exodus from Delhi continued, Harriet Tytler

Women, children, and wounded soldiers are attacked in this chilling depiction of the massacre at Cawnpore. The events pictured here did not occur simultaneously: The soldiers were killed first, the women and children two weeks later.

glanced behind her and through the growing darkness could see an angry red glow as fires set by the rioters spread through the cantonment, consuming the Tytlers' home and possessions. The British nightmare of a general revolt had finally come to pass. The Tytler family fled north, finally arriving in Ambala the next day, where friends provided temporary shelter.

Word of the rebellion spread across India. In Oudh, Indians affected by the British assumption of power, from court officials to displaced *taluqdars* (landed barons) to those with familial connections to the sepoys, joined forces at Lucknow. Fortunately for the British there, the new chief commissioner had the foresight to fortify the residency and stock it with provisions. Military and civilian Britons and the Indians loyal to them sought shelter there. Less fortunate were the British caught in Cawnpore, 50 miles southwest of Lucknow. The four Indian regiments there had rebelled. Under the leadership of a disaffected local noble, Nana Sahib (who as an adopted son had been a victim of the doctrine of lapse), they had trapped the British in a garrison neither well fortified nor

Hearing of the Indian uprising in May 1857, British troops hurry from the Himalayan foothills where they routinely spent the hot summer months, pushing southward by any means possible—horse, bullock cart, elephant, or shoe leather *(below)*. Four months afterward, following a grueling siege, British and loyal Indian soldiers fight their way through the streets of rebel-held Delhi against the defenders' furious barrage of rocks, bullets, and cannonballs *(right)*.

provisioned. Elsewhere, there were scattered uprisings in the Gangetic heartland and portions of the Punjab and the Deccan.

In Ambala, Robert Tytler learned that a relief force was being sent to retake Delhi, and he signed on as paymaster for the troops. As Harriet noted, "It was a perfect Godsend with three boys in England and everything we possessed lost in Delhi, even our last month's pay." For want of any alternative option, the captain proposed that Harriet and the children accompany him, thinking the city would be retaken in short order.

The field force of 3,400 British soldiers fought its way back to the ridge overlooking Delhi, where it halted. More rebels had flocked to the city since May, and the British attackers had too few men to take Delhi. At the same time, the field force would prove itself too strong to be dislodged from the ridge. It was a stalemate. Under the hot midsummer sun, the British troops camped out on the bare and stony heights. And Harriet waited to have her baby, sleeping out with her children in the cart in which they had traveled. "We had no home outside our cart. There we

Attended by a syce, or groom, a young boy and girl on their ponies pose in front of their country house—the very image of English gentry life. By the age of seven many well-to-do British children were shipped off to school in England and faced years of separation from their parents.

Bringing England to India

Although some Britons were fascinated by the mystery and splendor of India, the uprising—what the British called the Mutiny—of 1857 injected an element of fear into the colony, prompting the colonists to wear their Britishness more than ever like a cultural suit of armor. In a land far from home, amid customs, languages, and people that they viewed as exotic, the British strove to transplant and adapt the culture of their homeland to this alien soil.

They built private clubs for cricket, tennis, golf, and polo (this last sport adopted from Asia) and prohibited Indians from joining. While pursuing England's traditional passion for hunting, they chased Asian prey—tigers, bears, and boars—instead of foxes. Riding horses became such a symbol of Englishness that every member of Britain's civil service was required to be proficient in the saddle. And, seeking relief from spicy Indian cuisine, Britons eagerly gobbled canned foods sent from home. Though some colonials tried to establish a rapport with Indians, most of the British knew "the natives" only as servants, using them to create a pampered and lavish lifestyle they could not have enjoyed back in England.

A dazzling series of arabesque arches
frame the interior of this grand Indian
house, but its furnishings evoke the
atmosphere of an English drawing room.
The home belonged to an English couple in
southern India in the mid-1860s, and the
rococo-style furniture represented the height
of fashion in England at that time.

After a night of carousing—his clothes hastily pulled off and an unfinished glass of whiskey still within reach—an English officer is served coffee in bed by his Indian servant. Amateur photographer Willoughby Wallace Hooper composed this image of life in a British cantonment in the 1870s.

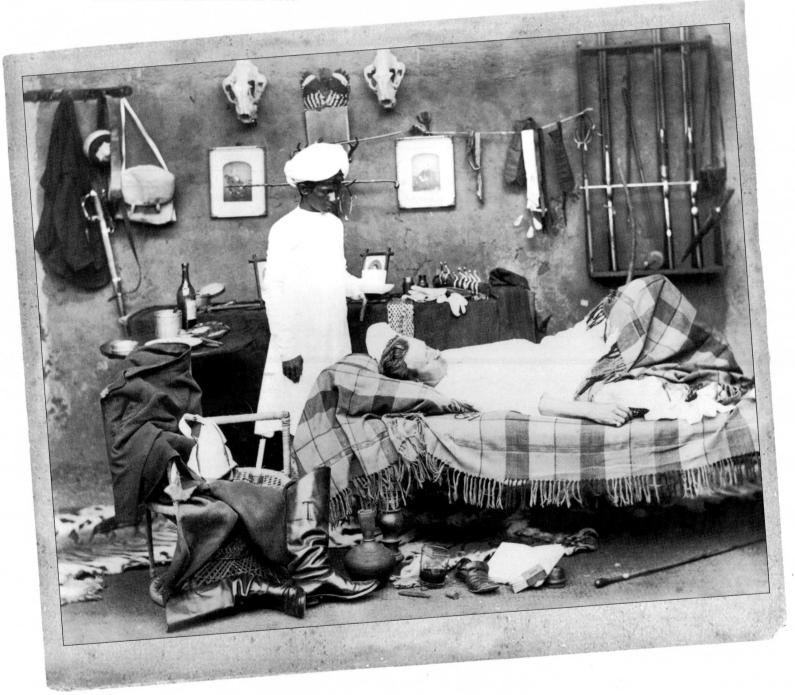

154

A group of Britons gather around their
trophy—a bear hunted down and killed with
a spear. Another favorite quarry was wild
boar. Hunters prided themselves on their
skill at pigsticking, which was carried out
on horseback and considered the greatest—as
well as one of the most dangerous—of
all sports in India.

A British traveler poses in front of a religious sculpture on a temple in Ceylon. Indian temples were a popular destination for British tourists, but escorts usually steered female sightseers away from the erotic art featured on some temple facades. One 19th-century guidebook advised women to tip local guides for not pointing out suggestive temple carvings.

Touring the Indian countryside for this group of Britons—including women, children, and dogs—required the service of over 20 servants and a number of elephants. Rugs have been laid and tables and chairs set up for their comfort. One travel writer recommended using "charming folding tables of bamboo and deodar [cedar]" while roughing it at camp.

GLOSSARY

Anglo-Indian: a person of British birth or ancestry living in India.

Ayah: an Indian nanny, lady's maid, or nurse.

Banian: an Indian agent responsible for handling, for a commission, business, household, and personal arrangements and affairs for the English living in India.

Barracks rats: name given to the soldiers' children who lived with their fathers and mothers in screened-off verandas in the soldiers' barracks.

Bengali: of or relating to the people, language, or culture of Bengal; a native of Bengal; the languages spoken in Bengal.

Bengh: bhang; an intoxicant obtained from hemp.

Black Hole of Calcutta: name for the detention cell in the military barracks in Calcutta where a number of East India Company employees died after being imprisoned there overnight by the nawab of Bengal.

Black Town: the segregated area where Indians and some other non-Europeans lived and traded.

Brahman: under the Hindu caste system, the highest ranking of the four varnas, responsible for performing priestly functions, studying and teaching the Vedas, and acting as advisers to rulers.

British Raj: the name for British-ruled India.

Budgerow: another name for a pinnace.

Bullock: a castrated bull; used in India as a pack animal or to pull carts loaded with cargo.

Bungalow: a one-story home, often with a veranda.

Burra khana: literally, big dinner or banquet.

Cantonment: a military installation in India.

Caste system: a system by which Hindu society was divided into four hierarchical groups, or varnas: Brahmans, kshatriyas, vaishyas, and shudras; outside the system were the untouchables.

Chabutara: literally, a terrace.

Courtier: one in attendance at a sovereign's court.

Curry: a food or dish seasoned with pungent spices.

Dandy: an oarsman.

Dastak: a trade license granted by a ruler, giving the right to trade without paying customs duties.

Dastur: a sum of money or gift, politely considered a commission, but in essence, a form of inducement for doing business or for favors.

Dhobi: a washerman; one who does laundry.

Dhoti: a long, cotton loincloth wrapped around the hips, with one end brought between the legs and fastened at the waist, worn by Hindu men.

Diwan: the financial officer of a province responsible for managing its revenue, collecting taxes, and remitting a portion to the Moghul imperial treasury; the power to collect taxes and administer a province.

Diwani: the chief financial officer of the Moghul empire; the right granted by the Moghul emperor to the East India Company under the Treaty of Allahabad to collect and keep the taxes in specific provinces; a tax collector or his assistant.

Durbar: a royal audience, reception, or ceremony to transact business, celebrate religious festivals, or mark important events held either publically in a large, ornate hall or privately, in a smaller, inner chamber, for relatives, councillors, ministers, and advisers.

East India Company: the British commercial enterprise chartered by the Crown in 1600 to trade with India. The company gradually became involved in and took over Indian political affairs, acting as an agent of British imperialism in India from the early 18th century until it was dissolved after the Indian uprising of 1857, when the British government assumed control over India.

Enfield rifle: a type of rifle that was easier to load than earlier guns, with the powder and bullet in a single, heavily greased paper cartridge, the end of which had to be bitten off before loading to expose the powder to the source of ignition.

Eunuch: a castrated man; in India, responsible for guarding the zenana.

Factor: an agent for the East India Company who bought goods for shipment to Britain and elsewhere.

Factories: name given to East India Company trading stations in the subcontinent that became, in essence, fortified warehouses surrounded by towns.

Fauj: army.

Firman: an edict or decree; a grant of privileges, such as, in the case of the East India Company, the right to trade and establish factories in India.

Gaddi: a highly decorative cushion placed on a low platform or a thronelike chair on which royalty sat.

Ghat: a broad flight of steps or a ramp leading down to a river, permitting easy access for bathing.

Golandar: in an East India Company army, one who carried ammunition; an artilleryman.

Governor general: under the Regulating Act of 1773, the ruling authority in British India.

Griffin: slang for a newcomer in India.

Gurkhas: a tribe of people in Nepal; the military force established by the ruling house of Nepal in the 17th century, known for its valor, loyalty, and ability to fight on difficult terrain; they were recruited by Britain into the ranks of the sepoys.

Half-caste: a person of Indian and European descent.

Harem: the women's quarters in a palace, used to house not only a man's wives, concubines, and young children, but all other female members of the household as well; also called a zenana; collectively, the name given to a man's wives, concubines, female relatives, and female servants living in a zenana.

Hindu: one who practices Hinduism.

Hindustani: one of the languages of northern India.

Hookah: a water pipe used for smoking tobacco, with a mouthpiece and a long tube passing through an urn filled with water, thus cooling the smoke from the tobacco, burned in an attached receptacle.

Hookah burdar: a servant who attends to a hookah.

Howdah: a rectangular, boxlike elephant saddle with low sides or railings and, usually, a decorative roof designed to protect the rider from rain and sun.

Indiaman: any large, sturdy trading ship with three masts working for the East India Company and varying in size from 400 to 1500 tons; usually heavily armed to protect its cargo and crew.

Jagir: a tax-free grant of land, along with its revenues, usually given only to high government officials, Brahmans, and military commanders but granted to the East India Company as well.

Jampan: a covered armchair carried by eight men.

Kansamah: a butler in an Anglo-Indian household.

Kari: a South Indian word for sauce.

Kedgeree: a curried casserole of smoked, flaked fish, boiled rice, and hard-boiled eggs; a popular part of the traditional English manor-house breakfast.

Khichri: a popular curried dish made of rice, lentils, and butter; the culinary inspiration for kedgeree.

Kimkhwab: Indian brocade woven entirely of gold and silver threads or of silk interwoven with gold or silver. Also called cloth of gold.

Kitmutgar: in English households in India, a person who served at the table.

Kookree: a curved knife carried by the Gurkhas.

Koran: the sacred text of Islam, the infallible word of Allah, as revealed to the prophet Muhammad; the primary source of Islamic law.

Kshatriya: under the Hindu caste system, the second of the four varnas, to which warriors belonged.

Laudanum: an alcoholic tincture made with opium, used at one time for medicinal purposes.

Lepcha: a member of a hill tribe living in Sikkim.

Mali: a gardener.

Maratha: a people of west-central India; a person who speaks the Marathi language; a loose confederation of Hindu rulers in west-central India whose soldiers were especially well trained and equipped.

Marquisate: the rank or territory of a marquess.

Masjid: a mosque.

Matchlock: a mechanical firing device developed in the 15th century and used for igniting gunpowder in hand-carried guns, such as muskets.

Memsahib: a title of respect for the mistress of a household; the female equivalent of sahib.

Minaret: a tower at a mosque from which the faithful are called to prayer.

Minbar: in Islamic religious architecture, the pulpit in a mosque from which the sermon is delivered.

Moghul: a Mongol; any of a group of primarily nomadic herding and hunting tribes from the steppes of central Asia, united under Chinggis Khan in the 14th century; a member of that group of Mongols who conquered India in 1526.

Moghul empire: the great imperial dynasty founded in 1526 by Babur, king of Kabul, with its capital at Agra; the empire ruled India until the 18th century, when England eroded its power but maintained its symbolic status as an empire until 1857, when the British exiled the last emperor.

Monsoon: a wind that changes direction with the season. In India, the summer monsoon blows from the sea and brings with it stifling heat and torrential rains, while the winter monsoon blows over land, bringing cool, dry air to the subcontinent.

Mosque: an Islamic house of prayer and, in many regions, the center of educational, political, social, and military functions as well.

Munshi: a language tutor.

Muslim: one who follows the teachings of Muhammad; an adherent of the Islamic faith.

Mussocks: buoyant floats made of inflated sheep hide on which men cavorted at the public baths.

Mussoola boats: a type of flat-bottomed boat.

Nabobs: name given to East India Company employees who prospered in India and flaunted their newly acquired wealth back in England.

Nawab: a Muslim ruler in the Moghul empire, usually either a provincial governor or prince.

Nizam: the title of the ruler of Hyderabad.

Olibanum: another name for frankincense, an aromatic gum resin valued for its oil; used both in worship and in medications.

Paijama: loose silk or cotton trousers with a drawstring waistband worn by Indian men and women and adopted by Britons, eventually becoming the inspiration for lounge pajamas and sleepwear.

Palanquin: a covered or enclosed litter, usually for one person, carried on curved bamboo poles on the shoulders of four or six bearers.

Pan: a slightly intoxicating mixture of areca nuts, lime, and spices, wrapped in a betel leaf and chewed to aid digestion.

Panchway: a vessel suitable for navigating India's shallow waterways, with a low-roofed shelter for protection from the sun and rain but no seats.

Pandit: a Brahman scholar or religious teacher.

Phaeton: a light, four-wheeled carriage containing one or two seats and drawn by a pair of horses.

Pike: a weapon consisting of a long wooden shaft with a pointed steel head, used as a naval boarding weapon by English seamen.

Pinnace: a houseboat powered by sails or by oarsmen. Also called a budgerow.

Privateer: an armed, privately owned ship author-ized by a government during wartime to prey upon, capture, or sink the war or merchant ships of the enemy or, during peacetime, those of pirates; the commander of such a ship.

Puggree: a light scarf or cloth wrapped around the head and worn as a turban.

Puja: Hindu ceremonial worship, ranging from simple, private daily prayers to elaborate temple rites and festivals, conducted by one or more priests, with its rituals varying widely depending on the occasion.

Punkah: a fan suspended from the ceiling, made either of a large palm frond or of cloth held in a large, rectangular frame, but in either case powered by a servant using a cord-and-pully system.

Purdah: in Islamic upper-class society, the seclusion of women from public view, using curtains or screens to protect their privacy inside buildings and heavy veiling when the women are out in public.

Raja: a Hindu ruler.

Rajput: a member of powerful Hindu landowning and military clans from northern and central India, said to be the descendants of both kings and the warrior ruling class.

Ramayana: one of India's two great religious epics.

Residency: in India, the compound where the resident and his staff lived and worked.

Resident: a British official attached to the court of an Indian ruler in a supposedly advisory, but often dominating, capacity.

Rupee: beginning in the late 1500s, the basic monetary unit of India, the value of which varied from region to region until it was standardized in 1835.

Sahib: title of respect equivalent to the English "sir" or "master"; a form of respectful address for a European or an Indian man of rank in colonial India.

Sanskrit: the ancient, classical language of India in which most of the texts of Hinduism were written and from which most of the languages spoken in northern India are derived.

Sari: an outer garment worn by women consisting of a single length of cotton or silk, five to seven yards long, most often worn with one end wrapped around the waist to form a skirt and the other draped over the shoulder and head.

Sati: the Hindu practice of burning widows alive on their husband's funeral pyres.

Sepoy: a Hindu or Muslim soldier armed and trained in the European manner by British officers, and serving, under British command, in native battalions in the army of the East India Company.

Shah: one of the titles given the Moghul emperor.

Shastras: sacred Hindu books that regulate religious, social, and professional behavior and activities.

Shudra: under the Hindu caste system, the fourth and lowest recognized varna, the servant and labor-ing class that served the three upper classes.

Sipahi: Persian word meaning soldier or horseman, from which the word sepoy is derived.

Stupa: originally, a simple, dome-shaped Buddhist funerary mound built to house a relic of the historic Buddha and his close associates but eventually evolving into more elaborate shapes.

Subahdar major: the senior Indian officer in a native infantry regiment of the British service.

Subaltern: a British officer equivalent to a lieutenant.

Syce: a stableman; a groom who took care of horses.

Taluqdars: Indian landed barons.

Tatties: screens placed over doors or windows and kept wet, made of cloth or woven vetiver grass, through which air could blow when placed on the windward side of the house to cool the interior.

Telugu: one of the Dravidian family of languages, spoken in southeastern and central India.

Thermantidote: a cooling device consisting of a cylinder fitted with dampened tatties and containing large, revolving fans; it stood against an exterior wall, with a funnel projecting into a room. Servants kept the tatties wet and turned the handles that moved the fans, forcing cooled air into the house.

Thuggee: ritual highway robbery and murder by strangulation, said to have been committed by a religious sect in honor of the goddess Kali.

Tutelary Deity: a god or goddess who serves as a guardian or protector.

Untouchables: under the Hindu caste system, those who fell outside the system, who performed tasks deemed too polluting for others and whose lives were bounded by numerous restrictions to prevent them from polluting members of the caste system.

Upanishads: Hindu religious and philosophical texts.

Vaishya: under the Hindu caste system, the third of the four varnas, considered to be commoners and consisting of farmers, merchants, and some artisans.

Varna: any of the four social classes or castes into which society was divided under the Hindu caste system, specifically, Brahman, kshatriya, vaishya, and shudra. A fifth group, the untouchables, was so low socially that it fell outside of the caste system.

Viceroy: the governor or ruler of a Crown colony, province, or country and the representative therein of the ruling sovereign.

Wherry: a small oar-propelled boat used to ferry back and forth from a pinnace to supply boats.

White Town: the segregated area of the city where the British and other Europeans lived.

Zenana: in either noble household, the women's quarters in a Hindu or Muslim palace, used to house not only a man's wives, concubines, and young children, but all other female members of the household as well. Also called a harem.

PRONUNCIATION GUIDE

Akbar-nama (UK-bur-NAH-muh)
Ajmer (uj-MEER)
Allahabad (ul-LAH-huh-BAHD)
Atmiya Sabha (AHT-MEE-yuh SUH-bhah)
Aurangzeb (OU-rung-ZEEB)
Baghmar (BAHGH-mahr)
Bahadur Shah (buh-HAH-dewr SHAH)
Baiza Bai (BEYE-za BEYE)
Balchand (BAHL-chund)
Bangla (BAHN-GLAH)
Banian (BAHN-yun)
Berar (bay-RAHR)
Berhampore (bayr-HUM-poor)
Betel (BEE-tul)
Bharatpur (BHAH-rut-poor)
Bihar (bi-HAHR)
Bijaigarh (bee-JEYE-gur)
Brahma (BRUH-hmah)
Brahman (BRAH-hmun)
Burhanpur (BUR-hun-poor)
Burra khana (bur-RAH KHAH-nuh)
Carnatic (kar-NAH-tik)
Chabutara (cha-BOO-tuh-RAH)
Chinsura (chin-SOO-rah)
Cuddalore (KOO-duh-loer)
Dharur (dhah-ROOR)
Dhobi (DHOE-bee)
Dhoti (DHOE-tee)
Dhuankund (dhew-AHN-kewnd)
Diwan (di-WAHN)
Diwan i khas (di-WAHN-i-KHAHS)
Doab (doe-WAHB)
Durbar (DUR-bahr)
Durga Puja (DUR-gah POO-jah)
Fatehgarh (FUH-tay-gar)
Fatehpur Sikri (FUH-tay-poor SEE-kree)
Gaja Raja Sahib (GUH-juh RAH-JAH SAH-hib)
Ganesha (guh-NAY-shuh)
Ganj-i-Sawai (GUNJ-i-sah-WEYE)
Ghat (ghaht)
Goanese (GO-uh-NEES)
Godavari (GO-DAH-vuh-REE)
Gopal Krishna Gokhale (GO-pahl KRISH-nuh GO-khuh-lay)
Gumti (GOOM-tee)
Gurkha (GOOR-khuh)
Haidar Ali (heye-dur UH-LEE)
Himalaya (hi-MAH-luh-yuh)

Hookah burdar (HEW-kah bur-DAHR)
Howdah (HOW-duh)
Hyat-ool-Nissa Begam (heye-ut-ewl-NIS-suh BAY-gum)
Hyderabad (HEYE-duh-ruh-bahd)
Idris (id-REES)
Jagannatha (juh-gun-NAH-tuh)
Jagat Seth (JUH-gut SAYT)
Jagir (juh-GEER)
Jahangir (juh-HAHN-geer)
Jahangiri Mahal (juh-HAHN-GEER-i muh-HUL)
Jaipur (JEYE-poor)
Jampan (JEM-pun)
Jemdanee (JUM-duh-nee)
Jubbulpore (JUB-bul-poor)
Jumna (JUM-nah)
Kabob (kuh-BAHB)
Kali (KAH-LEE)
Kalighat (KAH-LEE-ghaht)
Kanheri (kun-HAY-ree)
Kansamah (kahn-SAH-mah)
Kari (KAR-ree)
Karli (KAHR-lee)
Khichri (KHICH-ree)
Khurram (KHUR-rum)
Kimkhwab (kim-KHWAHB)
Kitmutgar (kit-mut-GAHR)
Koi hai (KOE-i HEYE)
Kookree (KEW-kree)
Kshatriyas (KSHUH-tree-yuhs)
Lepchas (LEP-chahs)
Maharaja Jai Singh (muh-hah-RAH-juh JEYE SING)
Mali (MAH-lee)
Manu (MUH-new)
Masjid (MUS-jid)
Meerut (MEE-rut)
Memsahib (MAYM-sah-hib)
Minbar (MIN-bahr)
Mir Jafar (MEER JUH-fur)
Mir Kasim (MEER KAH-sim)
Mirzapur (MEER-zuh-poor)
Mrityunjay (mri-TYEWN-jeye)
Mumtaz Mahal (MEWM-tahz muh-HUL)
Munshi (MEWN-shee)
Nabob (nuh-BAHB)
Nana Sahib (NAH-nah SAH-hib)
Nautch (nahch)
Nawab (nuh-WAHB)

Nilgiri (NIL-gi-ree)
Nizam (ni-ZAHM)
Nur Jahan (NOOR juh-HAHN)
Oudh (owdh)
Paijama (peye-JAH-mah)
Pan (pahn)
Pandit (PUN-dit)
Parwiz (pahr-VEEZ)
Peshawar (pay-SHAH-wur)
Prithiviraj ki jai (pri-thi-vee-RAHJ ki JEYE)
Puggree (PUG-gree)
Punjab (pun-JAHB)
Punkah (PUN-kah)
Puri (PEW-ree)
Raja (RAH-JAH)
Rajmahal (RAHJ-muh-HUL)
Rajput (RAHJ-pewt)
Ramayana (rah-MAH-yuh-nuh)
Ram Basu (RAHM BUH-sew)
Rammohan Roy (RAHM-MO-hun ROY)
Rath Yatra (RUT YAH-trah)
Rohilkhand (ROE-hil-khund)
Sahib (SAH-hib)
Sari (SAH-REE)
Sati (SUH-tee)
Serampore (SAY-rum-poor)
Seringapatam (say-RIN-guh-PUT-um)
Shah Alam (SHAH uh-LUM)
Shahjahanabad (SHAH-juh-HAH-nuh-bahd)
Shastra (SHAH-struh)
Shiva (SHI-vuh)
Shudras (SHOO-druhs)
Siraj-ud-Daula (SI-rahj-ewd-DOU-lah)
Stupa (STOO-puh)
Subahdar (SEW-bay-dahr)
Sundarbans (SEWN-dur-buns)
Surat (SOO-rut)
Taluqdar (TAH-lewk-dahr)
Tapti (TUP-tee)
Tarachandi (TAH-rah-CHUN-dee)
Thuggee (TUG-gee)
Trichinopoly (tri-chi-NAH-puh-lee)
Upanishads (EW-puh-ni-shuds)
Vaishyas (VEYE-shyus)
Varna (VAR-nuh)
Vedantic (vay-DAHN-tik)
Vedas (VAY-duhs)
Vilayat (vi-LEYE-ut)
Vishnu (VISH-new)
Vizagapatam (vi-SHAH-guh-puh-tum)

ACKNOWLEDGMENTS AND PICTURE CREDITS

ACKNOWLEDGMENTS

The editors wish to thank the following individuals and institutions for their valuable assistance in the preparation of this volume:

Terry Barringer, Special Collections, Cambridge University Library, Cambridge; Christopher Bayly, St. Catherine's College, Cambridge; Helen Compston, The Wakeman Trust, London; Patrick Conner, London; Anne-Marie Ehrlich, London; Rod Hamilton, Oriental and India Office Collections, British Library, London; Stephen Howe, Royal Armouries, Leeds, Yorkshire; Susan J. Mills, Regent's Park College, Oxford; Sarah Mitchell, Printed Book Reproductions, British Library, London; Chris Rawlings, Picture Library, British Library, London; Howard Simons, OIOC Reprographic Services, British Library, London; The Honourable Georgina Stonar, Oxfordshire; Marilyn Ward, Royal Botanic Gardens, Kew, Richmond, Surrey.

BIBLIOGRAPHY

BOOKS

Ali, B. Sheik. *Tipu Sultan: A Study in Diplomacy and Confrontation.* Mysore, India: Geetha Book House, 1982.

Andrews, Kenneth R. *Trade, Plunder and Settlement: Maritime Enterprise and the Genesis of the British Empire, 1480-1630.* Cambridge: Cambridge University Press, 1984.

Ansari, Muhammad Azhar. *Social Life of the Mughal Emperors, 1526-1707.* Allahabad: Shanti Prakashan, 1974.

Archer, Mildred:
British Drawings in the India Office Library (Vols. 1 and 2). London: H.M.S.O., 1969.
Company Drawings in the India Office Library. London: H.M.S.O., 1972.
Early Views of India: The Picturesque Journeys of Thomas and William Daniell, 1786-1794. London: Thames and Hudson, 1980.
India and British Portraiture, 1770-1825. London: Sotheby Parke Bernet, 1979.
India Observed: India As Viewed by British Artists, 1760-1860. London: Victoria and Albert Museum, 1982.
Natural History Drawings in the India Office Library. London: H.M.S.O., 1962.

Atkinson, George Francklin. *"Curry & Rice:" On Forty Plates.* New Delhi: Time Books International, 1982.

Banerjee, Samik. *Calcutta: 200 Years.* Calcutta: Tollygunge Club, 1981.

Barlow, Edward. *Barlow's Journal: Of His Life at Sea in King's Ships, East & West Indiamen & Other Merchantmen from 1659-1703* (Vol. 2). London: Hurst & Blackett, 1934.

Bayly, C. A.:
Empire and Information: Intelligence Gathering and Social Communication in India, 1780-1870. Cambridge: Cambridge University Press, 1996.
Indian Society and the Making of the British Empire (The New Cambridge History of India series). Cambridge: Cambridge University Press, 1988.

Beach, Milo Cleveland. *The Imperial Image: Paintings for the Mughal Court.* Washington, D.C.: Freer Gallery of Art, 1981.

Beatson, Robert. *Naval and Military Memoirs of Great Britain: From 1727 to 1783* (Vol. 1). Boston: Gregg Press, 1972.

Bence-Jones, Mark:
Clive of India. New York: St. Martin's Press, 1974.
Palaces of the Raj: Magnificence and Misery of the Lord Sahibs. London: George Allen and Unwin, 1973.

Botting, Douglas, and the Editors of Time-Life Books. *The Pirates* (The Seafarers series). Alexandria, Va.: Time-Life Books, 1978.

Brennan, Jennifer. *Curries and Bugles: A Memoir and a Cookbook of the British Raj.* New York: HarperCollins, 1990.

Brown, Judith M. *Modern India: The Origins of an Asian Democracy.* Delhi: Oxford University Press, 1985.

Brown, Michael F. *Itinerant Ambassador: The Life of Sir Thomas Roe.* Lexington: University of Kentucky, 1970.

Butler, Iris. *The Eldest Brother: The Marquess Wellesley, the Duke of Wellington's Eldest Brother.* London: Hodder and Stoughton, 1973.

Carey, Eustace. *Memoir of William Carey, D. D.* Hartford: Canfield and Robins, 1837.

Carey, W. H. *The Good Old Days of Honorable John Company.* Calcutta: Riddhi, 1980 (reprint of 1882 edition).

Chatterjee, Sunil Kumar:
Hannah Marshman: The First Woman Missionary in India. Sheoraphuli, Hoogly: Sri Sunil Chatterjee, 1987.
William Carey and Serampore. Calcutta: Ghosh, 1984.

Chaudhuri, K. N. *The Trading World of Asia and the English East India Company, 1660-1760.* Cambridge: Cambridge University Press, 1978.

Clive Museum. *Treasures from India: The Clive Collection at Powis Castle.* New York: Meredith Press, 1987.

Collet, Sophia Dobson. *The Life and Letters of Raja Rammohun Roy.* Ed. by Dilip Kumar Biswas and Prabhat Chandra Ganguli. Calcutta: Sadharan Brahmo Samaj, 1962.

Conner, Patrick. *George Chinnery, 1774-1852: Artist of India and the China Coast.* Woodbridge, Suffolk, England: Antique Collectors' Club, 1993.

Cordingly, David. *Under the Black Flag: The Romance and the Reality of Life among the Pirates.* New York: Random House, 1995.

Cotton, Evan. *East Indiamen: The East India Company's Maritime Service.* London: Batchworth Press, 1949.

Cutt, M. Nancy. *Mrs. Sherwood: And Her Books for Children.* London: Oxford University Press, 1974.

Das, Sisir Kumar. *Sahibs and Munshis: An Account of the College of Fort William.* Calcutta: Rupa, 1978.

Desmond, Ray, *The India Museum, 1801-1879.* London: H.M.S.O., 1982.

Dewanji, Malay. *William Carey and the Indian Renaissance.* Delhi: ISPCK, 1996.

The Dictionary of Art. New York: Grove, 1996.

Dodwell, Henry. *Dupleix and Clive: The Beginning of Empire.* London: Methuen, 1920.

Drewery, Mary. *William Carey: A Biography.* Kent, England: Zondervan, 1979.

Dupuy, R. Ernest, and Trevor N. Dupuy. *The Encyclopedia of Military History: From 3500 B.C. to the Present.* New York: Harper & Row, 1986.

Fay, Eliza. *Original Letters from India, 1779-1815.* London: Hogarth Press, 1986.

Fernandes, Praxy. *The Tigers of Mysore: A Biography of Hyder Ali & Tipu Sultan.* New Delhi: Viking, 1991.

Findly, Ellison Banks. *Nur Jahan: Empress of Mughal India.* New York: Oxford University Press, 1993.

Foster, William. *John Company.* London: John Lane the Bodley Head, 1926.

Frazer, Robert W. *British India.* Freeport, N.Y.: Books for Libraries Press, 1972 (reprint of 1896 edition).

Furber, Holden:
Private Fortunes and Company Profits in the India Trade in the 18th Century. Ed. by Rosane Rocher. Aldershot, Hampshire, England: Variorum, 1997.
Rival Empires of Trade in the Orient, 1600-1800. Minneapolis: University of Minnesota Press, 1976.

Gardner, Brian. *The East India Company: A History.* New York: Barnes & Noble, 1971.

Gascoigne, Bamber. *The Great Moghuls.* New York: Harper & Row, 1971.

Gibbs-Smith, C. H., comp. *The Great Exhibition of 1851.* London: H.M.S.O., 1950.

Godrej, Pheroza, and Pauline Rohatgi. *Scenic Splendours: India through the Printed Image.* London: British Library, 1989.

Gokhale, Balkrishna Govind. *Surat in the Seventeenth Century.* London: Curzon Press, 1979.

Golant, William. *The Long Afternoon: British India, 1601-1947.* New York: St. Martin's Press, 1975.

Goodwin, Peter. *The Construction and Fitting of the English Man of War, 1650-1850.* Annapolis, Md.: Naval Institute Press, 1987.

Greenberger, Allen J. *The British Image of India: A Study in the Literature of Imperialism, 1880-1960.* London: Oxford University Press, 1969.

Hibbert, Christopher. *The Great Mutiny: India 1857.* New York: Viking Press, 1978.

Hickey, William:
Memoirs of William Hickey. Ed. by Peter Quennell. London: Routledge & Kegan Paul, 1975.
Memoirs of William Hickey, 1790-1809 (Vol. 4). Ed. by Alfred Spencer. London: Hurst & Blackett, 1925.

Hoskins, Halford Lancaster. *British Routes to India.* New York: Octagon Books, 1966.

Husain, S. Abid. *The National Culture of India.* Bombay: Asia Publishing House, 1956.

Hutchins, Frances G. *The Illusion of Permanence: British Imperialism in India.* Princeton, N.J.: Princeton University Press, 1967.

Hutton, J. H. *Caste in India: Its Nature, Function, and Origins.* Cambridge: Cambridge University